ALSO BY GARE JOYCE

*Hockey Canada: Thirty Years of Going for Gold
at the World Juniors*

*The Devil and Bobby Hull: How Hockey's Original
Million-Dollar Man Became the Game's Lost Legend*

*Future Greats and Heartbreaks: A Year Undercover
in the Secret World of NHL Scouts*

The Only Ticket off the Island: Baseball in the Dominican Republic

*When the Lights Went Out: How One Brawl Ended
Hockey's Cold War and Changed the Game*

Sidney Crosby: Taking the Game by Storm

Novels by G. B. Joyce

The Code

The Black Ace

The Third Man In

Every Year a Parade Down Bay Street

YOUNG LEAFS

The Making of a
New Hockey History

GARE JOYCE

Published by Simon & Schuster

NEW YORK LONDON TORONTO SYDNEY NEW DELHI

SIMON &
SCHUSTER
CANADA

Simon & Schuster Canada
A Division of Simon & Schuster, Inc.
166 King Street East, Suite 300
Toronto, Ontario M5A 1J3

This Simon & Schuster Canada edition October 2018

SIMON & SCHUSTER CANADA and colophon are registered trademarks
of Simon & Schuster, Inc.

For information about special discounts for bulk purchases, please contact
Simon & Schuster Special Sales at 1-800-268-3216
or CustomerService@simonandschuster.ca.

Library & Archives Canada Catalog-in-Publication data

Joyce, Gare, 1956–, author
Young Leafs : the making of a new hockey history / Gare Joyce.
Previously published by Simon and Schuster Canada in 2017.
ISBN 978-5011-6992-2 (softcover)
1. Toronto Maple Leafs (Hockey team). 2. National Hockey League.
3. Hockey players—Ontario—Toronto. I. Title.
GV848.T6J69 2018   796.962'6409713541   C2018-901013-4

Manufactured in the United States of America

1   3   5   7   9   10   8   6   4   2

ISBN 978-1-5011-6987-8
ISBN 978-1-5011-6992-2 (pbk)
ISBN 978-1-5011-6991-5 (ebook)

*To King Clancy, Pat Burns, and Pat Quinn, three Hockey
Hall of Famers I met going back to the Gardens.
Yeah, I know, if only you had these kids to work with.*

YOUNG
LEAFS

PROLOGUE

A ROOKIE FORWARD NAMED JAKE GUENTZEL SLOWED TO A stop along the boards on the right wing, seemingly innocently enough. He had a poor angle, no room, and no view of the Toronto Maple Leafs net. Another rookie, a defenceman from Moscow named Nikita Zaitsev, stood directly in front of Guentzel, had him locked up and shut down. And behind Zaitsev was forty feet of open ice to the Toronto net, where goaltender Curtis McElhinney watched what looked like nothing much unfold. Guentzel threw the puck towards the net, a what-the-hell-why-not shot. Guentzel's shot wasn't a hard one—not even a shot at all, really—but it pinballed like it had eyes. First it deflected off Zaitsev's right skate and was heading well wide of the net—at least until Zaitsev's partner on defence, Jake Gardiner, facing McElhinney, tried to kick it up to his stick. At the very moment the puck hit Gardiner's skate you could see it in Gardiner's posture: reflexive regret. He realized he couldn't get his stick on the puck in time. Worse, McElhinney was on the other side of the net, giving him little chance to get back in position. He pushed hard to his right and seemed to have it covered, but then the puck slid between his legs, trickling over the goal line, not even moving fast enough to reach the back of the net.

That made the score Pittsburgh 3, Toronto 2. It was the 238th goal given up by the Leafs in the season. And yet Guentzel's goal, the one that came in Game 81, the second-to-last of the season, was the stuff that heartbreak is made of, this time enriched by psychic plutonium. The stakes were higher that night than they had been all season long. With a win—a desperately needed win—the Leafs would be through to the postseason. With a loss in regulation, well, it wouldn't be over, but it would look bleak, to say the least.

There were thirteen minutes to go in the game. It was 9:30 A.M. Eastern Standard Time, but the Toronto Maple Leafs' season neared midnight.

A sense of dread pervaded the crowd, from the platinum seats where swells dropped $500 a head on a night's entertainment to the very upper bowl, the 300 level, where a diehard on an economy plan might be able to get away with a C-note and change. As McElhinney pulled the puck from the back of the net, a collective thought bubble hung above the crowd: *Again.* Those fans who led a more deeply self-examined life only used that as a starting point. They had to question all that had come before. *Was it all just a horrific tease, some grim, existential joke?* A tortuous winter had led to this seemingly torturous end as spring was on the city. Now they could see the grand and awful design, that their team should go down, that it would be a self-inflicted wound, that all those good things from the eighty previous games would be kicked away. *We have met the laughingstock, and it is us. Again.*

In other recent seasons, fans had known few good times and inevitable despair. Just one year earlier, it might not have even risen as high as despair—it had started with losing and ended the same way, rarely interrupted with any good turns as the team finished last in the NHL. Fans were so practiced in losing, they couldn't be bothered to boo. This season, though, had been a ride. An uneven one, yes. As always, there had been some tough nights. But still, in thirty-nine previous home games, the team had lost in regulation only twelve times, and in the previous month, they had been making a push to the playoffs.

So much promise, and then Guentzel's goal made the prospect of the season not lasting twenty-four more hours all too real. Over the winter, something amazing had seemed to be within the team's grasp. But over the season's last week, it had been slipping away.

The producer was in the ear of the cameramen for a *Hockey Night in Canada* broadcast, who knew to look for a crowd reaction. He zoomed in on one towheaded kid, bent over in his seat, his head fully buried in his hands. His anguish was well beyond his years, just a grade schooler, likely one whose father wasn't alive when the Leafs won the Cup back in '67, yet somehow representative of all Maple Leafs fans.

The dread at the Air Canada Centre gave off a low-grade electric hum. The crowd hadn't sounded this way all year. The likes of it hadn't really been heard since the arena was raised—this dashed-hopes fusion of shortness of breath, hearts skipping a beat, and flop sweat. The hush that fell over the arena allowed those in the 300 level to hear the puck hit the blades of sticks and players' voices calling out.

It wasn't so complicated on the ice.

Things never are, really. The home team with everything to play for was trailing the defending Stanley Cup champions, who had nothing to play for. The home team was a young team. For a couple, this was the first Game 81 of their career; for others, not much more than that. The champions were practiced at this stuff. They were priming themselves, reloading for a deep run into spring.

The home team had an array of precocious talent, including a young player who was the consensus favourite to win the Calder Trophy, the award that goes to the league's best rookie. This was all new, and maybe, in just getting this far, they had shot their bolt.

The away team had rested several players in advance of the playoffs, but Sidney Crosby, the two-time Hart Trophy winner and two-time Olympic gold medalist, was not one of them. Nor was Phil

Kessel, who had been the Leafs' most convenient scapegoat for six seasons until he'd been traded a couple of summers before.

You had to wonder what the NHL schedule-makers had been thinking when they drew up the last week of the season for the Maple Leafs, a frantic race to the finish, five games in seven nights. Every team would have had a patch or two like this, a ridiculous compression of the schedule to accommodate the World Cup back in the fall and the weeklong midseason break that all teams get thanks to lobbying from the NHL Players' Association. It was simply the Leafs' dumb luck that their worst rush would be at season's end.

Of course, the schedule-makers likely assumed that the league would have sorted itself out by the end of the season. Those who had a shot at a Stanley Cup would have emerged, and those who were looking to land in the lottery would have been long submerged. On the former count, yes, things had been mostly sorted out—seven teams in each conference were in, with Pittsburgh, of course, among them for the eleventh season in a row. The Leafs, however, were precipitously on the bubble that Saturday night.

Every time the puck was dropped throughout the last two or three months, the Leafs had heard that *this* was their biggest game of the season. They had heard it as recently as two nights before, when they lay down against Tampa Bay, a game they wanted to believe was an aberration.

Over the next five minutes, the Leafs rolled over the boards and looked punched out, like a boxer grown arm-weary. They seemed overtaken by events: five full minutes without a whistle, up and back and up and back, six line changes and counting, coach Mike Babcock rolling all four lines, trying to squeeze an extra shift for Auston Matthews.

The hum gradually gave way to silence. Nineteen thousand people, and not a shout to be heard. No horn blowing. No cheers, no "Go Leafs Go." The crowd turned utterly still, not like an arena so much as a waiting room.

With eight and a half minutes left, the whistle finally blew, and Pittsburgh defenceman Mark Streit took a penalty for hauling down Leo Komarov behind the Penguins' net. Even on the power play, though, the Leafs were flat. Somehow they kept possession and applied some pressure, but a little of the fine touch had gone out of the game. Time was winding down. The shots on goal in the third period told the story of the game's direction: Pittsburgh 2, Toronto 9.

After Streit was let out of the box, the game clock seemed to speed up. For a team and its fans, the seconds never come off fast enough when holding a lead. With the season in the balance, it felt like the clock had been put on fast forward. A cheer of "Go Leafs Go" sounded mournful, like "Danny Boy" going up at a wake, and as tired as the team being urged on.

Some souls, hardened by so many bad turns over the years, had already moved past this game—check that—this season. Just a couple of weeks ago, fans talked optimistically about the Leafs opening the playoffs at home. And then came the fade to black. Fans had seen this movie before. In 2012, it had come in a 1-9-2 streak in February that dropped them out of the playoffs and had then-GM Brian Burke comparing the team to "an eighteen-wheeler going right off a cliff." A couple of years later, it was eight consecutive losses that snuffed out a shot at the playoffs. This time it seemed like it would be this four-game home stand in the very last week of the season.

What would be the postmortem? A young team that had run out of gas, yes; with the benefit of hindsight and rewrite, everyone saw that coming. Maybe it would be an optimistic spin: When this team finally comes together, they'll make it happen at moments like this. They'll know what to do.

It had been a remarkable season just to get to this point, one that made history on several counts. Individual records. Team records. No one had seen it coming. If there was hope of extending the season, it was going to take one more improbable turnaround. Was it too much to ask? If you were too old and had seen it fall short, then yes, to hope was to laugh. You'd have to be young and blissfully innocent to believe that one more goal or one more win was still out there.

With less than six minutes left the puck came back to Streit on the point, and he let loose. Brian Boyle, the fourth-line centre and the Leaf veteran who had been in this do-or-die moment most often before, dropped to one knee and took a shot in the leg. Stinging, still kneeling, Boyle pushed the puck ahead to Kasperi Kapanen, who skated into the neutral zone. Behind the play Boyle flexed his leg and skated to the bench for a line change, and Matthews hopped onto the ice in his place. The Leafs got the puck deep and began working the cycle along the boards in Pittsburgh's zone. With a burst of speed, Matthews carried the puck behind the goal line, all eyes on him. Leafs defenceman Matt Hunwick dropped in from the point, and Matthews hit him with a pass. Hunwick stretched to collect the puck and wasted no time, sliding a no-look pass through the slot. The puck landed right on the tape of Kapanen's stick, and he wired it into the back of the net.

The crowd erupted as the Leafs players mobbed an ecstatic Kapanen, who, in his sixteenth NHL game, had his first goal, his first point. The players on the bench patted each other's helmets in congratulations as the coaching staff pumped their fists. Fans who had just seconds before been resigned to their fate suddenly were on their feet, leaping and hugging—the ACC had new life.

There was just one problem. The game was still tied. As the adrenaline wore off and the teams reset for the face-off, reality set in. The Leafs hadn't saved their season or suddenly secured their chances of a playoff spot—they'd just given it a jolt from the crash cart to keep hope's heart beating. There were five minutes left, and Toronto still needed its win.

The Leafs had an open casting call for heroes. Some of the candidates had answered such calls before. Many hadn't. Most, actually.

CHAPTER ONE

IT SHOULD HAVE STARTED ON A SATURDAY NIGHT, THE TRADI-
tional slot for *Hockey Night in Canada,* especially as it featured
two Canadian teams, the Leafs and the Ottawa Senators, locked
in a fierce rivalry. And it should have started in Toronto, at least if
seniority matters, which it should, given that the Leafs were entering into their centenary season (more than that if you go back to
the franchise's antecedents, the Arenas and the St. Pats). But it was
a Thursday night in Ottawa, a quirk of the schedule-maker in the
league's Manhattan offices, one insensitive to drama and history and
all things Canadian.

Then again, maybe the league's decision was better thought out
than presumed. The game was anticipated by two sets of loyal fans,
although expectations were mixed. The Senators had made the playoffs the year before, and their prospects for the season ahead were
mixed: A new GM, Pierre Dorion, had taken over for a longtime
head man, Bryan Murray, who had managed the team while battling
incurable colon cancer. And the Leafs, well, the prospects were not
high enough to be described as mixed. The team had finished last
overall in the league the season before, laughably so, and although it
felt like the teardown was ongoing, management was actively selling
the theme of "rebuilding."

Most assumed that the 2016–17 season would be a painful process for the Maple Leafs. At its best, it would be a cold introduction

to the man's game for a flight of young players, and as many as ten players in the lineup this season would qualify as rookies. At its worst, it might devolve into a brutal initiation, trial by ordeal for fresh-faced kids. They were breaking into the league surrounded by several veteran survivors of the *annum horribilis*. The rookies in the line-up for Game 1 in Ottawa fell into tiers. Connor Brown and Zach Hyman were forwards who had spent enough time in the organization to establish ceilings—they both had a good shot at sticking around as industrial-strength depth players in the NHL, but you wouldn't win with them on your top two lines. Nikita Zaitsev was an almost unknown commodity—a never-drafted, twenty-five-year-old defenceman who had toiled in the KHL for six seasons, playing virtually his entire career in the shadows before signing a one-year deal as a free agent with Toronto in the summer. These, though, were the members of the supporting cast. Driving the interest in the team were the first-round draft picks from the three preceding Junes, those around whom the Leafs management had planned to build a contender, those in whom Toronto fans placed hope—a questionable investment in recent years.

William Nylander had been taken eighth overall in the 2014 draft. The son of former NHLer Michael Nylander made cameo appearances with the team in training camp as an eighteen-year-old before going back to Sweden for a season to play alongside his father before committing to a season with the Marlies, Toronto's American Hockey League affiliate. In the AHL, Nylander established himself as one of the most skilled players in a league that was usually tough on teenagers. His play was good enough for him to be called up to the big club for a few weeks in the spring. It was a taste of things to come, but the team's intention was still to shelter Nylander in the minor-league club, distancing him from the stormy "tanking-for-No. 1" season and protecting him from being indoctrinated into a team culture that accepted, or even tacitly approved of, losing.

Mitch Marner had been the fourth overall pick in 2015, and although his puck skills were at times magical, questions lingered: Could a player that slight step into the league at nineteen and physically endure the big hits? So many young players get hurt—some severely—after being thrown in before they matured. The most cited example was Gilbert Brulé, a fifth overall pick of Columbus in 2005, who wound up with a broken sternum and seemed to never recover. Marner was a forward in Brulé's physical mold, listed at five-eleven and 170 pounds, numbers that seemed generous when you saw him in person. Still, if Nylander had little to learn in the AHL, Marner had nothing whatsoever to gain from a return to major junior. His London Knights team had won the Memorial Cup the spring before, laying waste to every team that got in their way. For his part, Marner came away with all the major Player of the Year awards, and his line with the Knights, Christian Dvorak and Matthew Tkachuk, had broken long-standing league scoring records. As a junior-age player, Marner couldn't be sent to the AHL because of an agreement between the NHL and the Canadian Hockey League. Could he stick with the big club? Would it be better to put him at wing rather than centre to avoid injury? The answers would become clear pretty quickly.

Those questions were not there when it came to how or where Auston Matthews would be used. The first overall pick of the 2016 draft, Matthews had spent the full previous season playing in the Swiss pro league. He had already skated and starred with the U.S. national team at the world championships that spring. He had played with Connor McDavid, Jack Eichel, and other young stars on Team North America at the World Cup. There was no other place to play Matthews but at centre and with the big club. Still, pundits and fans figured that the team would take a cautious approach: Give him second- or third-line minutes, give him a bit more of a workload as the season played out. The prevailing wisdom: Mike Babcock will be teaching—emphasize *teaching*—Matthews the NHL game.

That was before the opener in Ottawa. Within sixty minutes, the presumed narrative for the season would be sent to rewrite and the prevailing wisdom would be shredded.

On his third shift, Matthews went hard to the Senators' net and tried to get off a shot on goaltender Craig Anderson. Ottawa's Derick Brassard got to Matthews before he could let loose, locking up the rookie and lifting his stick. Matthews fought through the check and kept possession of the puck, throwing a backhand pass to Nylander, who had taken a position behind the net. Nylander threw the puck over to Hyman, who sent a pass back to Matthews. Matthews finished the sequence by snapping the puck past Anderson for the first goal of his career, the first goal of the game, and the first goal of the Leafs' season.

As first career goals went, it was an auspicious one but hardly unprecedented. You wouldn't have put Matthews's up there with Mario Lemieux, who, on his first career shift, stripped future Hockey Hall of Famer Ray Bourque of the puck at the blueline for a clear breakaway, ate up the length of the ice in what seemed like six strides, and cleanly deked Boston goalie Pete Peeters. Matthews's first was, by comparison, not so dramatic, and it was in no way single-handed. It was just a piece of the game circa 2016, a product of body position and puck possession around an opponent's net. It lacked beauty. It lacked magic. It was just a goal, indistinguishable from hundreds in an NHL season.

This, however, could not be said of Matthews's second goal, the one for which his first game will be long remembered, the one that will become part of league lore.

Up on press row, pro scouts from ten NHL teams took their assigned seats. They had their ringed notebooks out and had written down the line combinations in the pregame. They had made one-line, even one-word notations beside Matthews's name after that first goal. The home side had scored twice, to make the game 2–1, and to the dispassionate pros doing other teams' intel, it was looking like a fairly unremarkable early season contest. That changed with just under six minutes left in the first period.

Matthews bore down on Senators forward Mark Stone, who controlled the puck at the Ottawa blueline. Matthews pushed the veteran Stone off the puck with almost casual ease, but found Stone's linemate Mike Hoffman bearing down on him. It looked like Matthews would have just momentary possession, like he'd be well advised to dump the puck into the Ottawa end if he had a chance, just to chase it again or get a line change. Instead, Matthews stickhandled and pushed the puck between Hoffman's skates and blew by him, albeit southbound, in retreat, back towards the centre red line. It looked like he was skating straight at Kyle Turris, another veteran and the centre between Hoffman and Stone, who gave chase, hustling to back-check. Matthews pivoted without stopping and crossed the Ottawa blueline on his far left wing. Turris, skating as hard as he could, couldn't catch up. Then, without looking to his right, Matthews caught a glimpse of Hoffman in his peripheral vision and ducked—Hoffman went to shove Matthews's helmeted head into the glass but just lunged and punched air with two hands.

Matthews pushed hard away from the boards to avoid a linesman who was pressed against the glass and waving the play onside. The puck was just beyond the reach of Matthews's stick, and Ottawa defenceman Erik Karlsson took possession to clear the puck, weighing his options. Matthews used a quick fake—a tap of his stick to Karlsson's left side—to sucker the two-time Norris Trophy winner. He then lifted Karlsson's stick and found himself with a clear path to the Senators' net, though it was on an angle sharper than 45 degrees. Karlsson's partner on the blueline, Marc Methot, slid in skates-first from the far side in a desperate attempt to block the anticipated shot, but he was a beat too late. Matthews wired the puck past Anderson on the short side.

The sequence took over nine seconds from the start to the red light. The play drew both cheers from Toronto fans who had made the trek to Ottawa and gasps from those in the seats, no matter what their allegiances. No, it wasn't Matthews's first goal, but still it was a first-game memory that would be up there with Mario Lemieux's. Six Senators had had a shot at Matthews—one of them had a pair of chances—and he had gone past and through them all, with a linesman to boot.

There had been no cheers from the scouts after the first goal, no words exchanged. A few raised eyebrows; some cracked their poker faces and jotted down notes beside No. 34 in reports that would be filed in the morning. On the second goal, though, the reaction was a little more emphatic: "He could be okay," one quipped.

One veteran working the game had been an amateur scout for more than a decade before he flipped to the pro side, just before Matthews landed at the U.S. National Team Development Program (USNTDP) in Ann Arbor, Michigan. The scout had only casually watched Matthews playing at the world juniors the two previous seasons. He heard Matthews's name discussed in his team's war room in advance of the draft, although not in any serious way, given that his team had made the playoffs and had no shot at landing Matthews.

Scouts won't make definitive player evaluations based on what they call "limited viewing"—that is, a handful of games. Even four or five games might be an insufficient window into a player's game. After the first period of Matthews's NHL career, the scout didn't hesitate to pass judgment: "I'm coming in it with fresh eyes," the veteran scout said. "I try to do that with any young player—you know, not to rely on what I've heard or any of the hype. I'm probably even more skeptical with a kid who is hyped. I'm thinking that whatever they're saying, it's exaggerated. It doesn't mean anything until you've done it in the league . . . until you showed me. And he showed me."

All that said, there were eighty-one more games left in the season. Two more periods left in the opener. Who knew what else Matthews might show?

Dave Pal was 450 kilometres away from the game, but he was watching it no less intently than the scouts up on press row. It would be hard or heartless to call Dave Pal an amateur. An NHL scout will miss a game or two a season for whatever reason—it might be illness, a flight cancellation, an anniversary, a kid's big day. Pal had a full-time job and a life to lead, but he'd still missed only one Leafs game in the last twenty-five years, and that only under the most extenuating of circumstances. "It was the big blackout a few years back and it was freezing out," Pal says. "I actually had my generator down from the cottage for whatever reason. I could have run it, I guess, to watch the game, but my grandmother's place was freezing, so while the game was going on, I was getting the heat on at her place."

Likewise, it would have been hard-hearted to judge those at his flank as anything less than professional. They lined the bar at TKO's, a tavern on the Danforth in Toronto's east end. TKO's advertises itself as a Leafs joint, and Pal and his pals are its constituency: No one needs to get carded here. These are mature adults. They have known victories and losses in life. A majority of them were alive when the Leafs won the Cup and have faint memories of it, even though less than 30 percent of Canadians can make that claim. Their memories grow more vivid with more recent history—John Brophy and Wendel Clark in the 1980s, and Pat Burns and Doug Gilmour in the '90s. They had come here since Clark's rookie season, not long after the bar opened. They had watched Gilmour's Leafs get tantalizingly close to making the final against Montreal in 1993. They had convened in this place on game nights for a few communal close brushes and far more disappointments in the two decades since.

The demographic of the crowd at TKO's changed as Pal and his friends grew older, and their ranks thinned by circumstance—some moving away, a couple of others giving up drinking after beating back illness, one after a bout with cancer, another a heart attack. "Life has a way of getting in the way," Pal said.

So, too, did technology, as far as business at TKO's went. Big-screen television viewing became accessible at home, replicating and even improving the experience at the bar, without the pools, without the side bets, without the bell ringing for Leafs goals. Even the franchise had horned in on the communal viewing of games—the most memorable image of the team's last big heartbreak, the blown third-period lead in Game 7 against Boston in 2013, was not goaltender James Reimer facedown on the ice, as if looking to tunnel his way out of the arena. No, the image that sticks was the wide shot of thousands of young fans gathered outside the ACC, watching the game on a massive high-definition screen in Maple Leaf Square. To ownership at TKO's and sports bars across the city, those inconsolable kids were a lost generation of patrons.

Through to the start of the second period in Ottawa, the broadcast featured no shots of Maple Leaf Square—if producers had planned shots of the mob scene outside the ACC, they were scrubbed in favour of replays and analysis of Matthews's two goals. Chatter at TKO's focused on the same. "He's on pace for . . . what's six times eighty-two?" said a regular known only as Ghostly Bob.

The waitress rang the bell twice more in the second period, both times for Matthews goals.

The first came barely a minute in. Morgan Rielly had the puck on the left side of the ice, with no great options. Four Senators packed into the slot and the ice below, and there were no clear lanes to shoot through or skate into. At least, that's how it looked until Matthews slipped into the space between defencemen Dion Phaneuf, the former Leafs captain, and Cody Ceci—how they let Matthews through without so much as a stick touching him is a question they had to be asking themselves after he took a pass from Rielly and, in a blink, fired it past Anderson. Twenty-one minutes into his NHL career, the rookie had a hat trick.

As Matthews's linemates mobbed him and hats rained onto the ice, TKO's achieved a bedlam unseen since the Leafs carried that three-goal lead late in Game 7 in Boston a thousand heartbreaks ago. Each patron smiled and laughed and floated like he had hit the lottery.

So it went for another eighteen minutes of play, and then the improbable crossed over into the impossible. Matthews skated hard to the net on a two-on-one with Nylander carrying the puck down the right wing. Matthews beat defenceman Chris Wideman to the goalmouth and rerouted a slick pass from Nylander with one touch, cleanly beating Anderson and barely beating the clock, which had run down to 0:03.

"This has to be a joke," Dave Pal says. "This is the twilight zone."

Says Ghostly Bob: "I hope I live long enough to see how this turns out."

Nick Fatsis, the owner of the bar, rings the bell at the end of the period, his adrenaline pumping not only because of the historic happenings in Ottawa but also for his much-improved business prospects on the Danforth.

"This is almost too good to be true," the proprietor says.

Fatsis was right—the night wasn't entirely pulled from a storybook. Maybe it was all too much to ask for a team that was leaning on six rookies, three of them playing in their first NHL game, too much to ask of a line-up so dramatically changed from one season to the next. Ottawa came back to tie the game in the third period. Leafs management had traded a first-round pick and a few other pieces to Anaheim for goaltender Frederik Andersen over the summer, and in his debut with the club, he gave up a couple of weak goals to send the game into overtime. Maybe Babcock got caught up in the moment as well, sending Matthews out to take the face-off at the start of the three-on-three overtime—a half minute later, Karlsson got payback for his earlier embarrassment, shaking Matthews and going through the back door for the winning goal.

Auston Matthews became the first NHLer to score four goals in his NHL debut and the youngest player in league history to score four goals in a game, but still the Leafs came away with just one point. If this was the start of a new era, then the new era was still looking for its first W. On that night, those who derided Toronto as the Centre of the Universe and the Leafs as a cosmic joke probably felt like they had the last laugh. *It had to go wrong. It's the Leafs.*

If a player's history, his route to the NHL, doesn't entirely define his talent, it at least provides a window into its evolution and explanation of how it came to be. It hangs out there in NHL history and is woven into the fabric of the game's lore. When people talk about Gordie Howe, they inevitably retell the stories of how, at age thirteen, he worked with grown men, hauling hundred-pound bags of cement on summer work crews in Saskatoon. With Bobby Hull, it's skating seven miles along frozen Lake Ontario from the company town of Point Anne to Belleville to play in peewee games. With Bobby Orr, it's skating on frozen ponds around Parry Sound with older players in town. With Wayne Gretzky, it's skating on a sheet of ice in his backyard, flooded by his hockey-playing father, Walter, and watching *Hockey Night in Canada,* tracing the puck around the television screen.

It's no different with today's stars, although the new stories seem a little more structured: Sidney Crosby going to Shattuck–St. Mary's, the Minnesota private-school hockey hothouse where every waking hour is seemingly school, homework, or hockey; Alexander Ovechkin coming up through the sports school of Moscow Dynamo, the organization headed up by his mother, an Olympic gold medallist in basketball.

Strength, skill, endurance, and resolve emerge in youth, and you can see trends and patterns there. Not all the stories are exactly the same, but common threads run through them. And you can see in their rise precisely how their talents emerged—Howe with his strength, Gretzky with his eerie prescience, Crosby with his never-a-wasted-second approach to play and life.

Auston Matthews's backstory is not quite a stand-alone, but it's close. He came from just about the least likely place of all, following in no one else's skate path. And just as his talent is separate and distinct, even hard to define, there's an aspect of *otherness*—he gets things done on the ice, but exactly how is not always clear and is often wholly unexpected.

What sets Matthews apart defies easy explanation, even for those who played with and against him. It's not there in a physical aspect. It's not that he's so much stronger—at least not now, at age nineteen—like Howe; not that he's so much faster like Orr, although he would surely rank in the elite and will only rise as he matures. But nor is it there as a piece of character: He's not so driven as Crosby, a near-ascetic type-A personality; not that he's more focused than the predatory, reckless Ovechkin, the ultimate disrupter. Matthews is a contrast to both. Off the ice, he's a relaxed, laid-back kid. On the ice, he's a player whose game reflects a sense of order and control.

If anything, Matthews borrows from Gretzky, though to say so is to lob a live grenade at a young prospect. Still, it's not a huge stretch to say that he played in something roughly the same size as a backyard and that he sees the game like a kid tracking the puck around the television screen, seeing not just where the puck has gone but where it's going next.

"He doesn't just see what's in front of him. He sees what's ahead of him . . . how things are going to unfold," said Ryan Shannon, a former NHLer who played against Matthews in his last season before joining the Maple Leafs. "He's not taking chances or gambling. He knows. We said it was like the puck follows him around the ice."

It goes by a bunch of labels. *Anticipation* is a popular one; *vision* also. In the parlance of NHL scouts, *hockey sense* gets tossed around. But that's praise heaped on a player who knows what to do in a given situation, a player who doesn't get lost on the ice, who plays within the game's conventions. Gretzky possessed something else: a sense of what others would do, teammates and opponents both. On his first trip through the league, Matthews has dropped significant hints that he might possess the same gift. Even on his first NHL goal, when it seemed he didn't carry the puck through four Ottawa Senators so much as it *followed* him, it was clear that Matthews had a talent of a different sort.

The comparison of players through the ages is purely a mug's game. The NHL has evolved dramatically and necessarily over the years. The rules have had to change ahead of the players, ahead of the coaches. How a star's skills would translate from one era to the next is simply speculative, never more than one person's guess and another's derision. That the very best players would adapt, however, seems like a fair shot. Gretzky played at a time when the pace of the game and the size of players allowed him to possess the puck. Now any given sixty minutes of NHL action is played at a dead, unbroken sprint and boils down to a thousand mano a mano situations, each player trying just to hold on to the puck or to gain possession of it. Analysts talk about "winning puck battles" or "winning fifty-fifty pucks," and those who win most will most often come away with two points. In any given game that Auston Matthews plays in, you can watch him chase a puck, especially in the opponent's end, and you'll presume that he has no better than half a chance to come away with it. And yet, when you presume that he doesn't have a real shot at it, that his chase is almost certainly in vain, he still comes up with it—not every time, but more often than can be credited to dumb luck.

It's nothing you can come away with by chance, no matter how many bags of cement you lift, how many miles on a frozen lake you skate, how many extra assignments you take on at a prep school hockey factory or years you put in at a state-sponsored sports academy. Yes, you can teach a young player the rudimentary skill of playing without the puck; it will be drilled home when he reaches the elite age-group ranks and hammered into him as a young pro. Matthews is way ahead of his class on that count, but more than that, he displays a talent for denying opponents a puck that they are accustomed to holding on to. "It's hard to say what it is, but I know it's either there or it isn't," Ryan Shannon said.

In the end, Matthews's is a hard-to-define talent, and his

backstory goes only halfway to explaining it, a fact that only makes the riddle more intriguing.

Though it felt like Matthews had come from out of the middle of no-where, hockey had been in the Southwest long before him. The Phoenix Apaches played a season in the semipro California Hockey League in the late 1950s before folding. The Victoria Maple Leafs of the minor-pro Western Hockey League moved to Phoenix and became the Roadrunners in 1967. The Roadrunners won league championships in 1973 and '74 and were led by, among others, Howie Young, a talented hothead with a drinking problem who had been packed off into exile by the NHL. The franchise's success helped Phoenix establish a fran-chise in the World Hockey Association. That team took the Roadrun-ners nickname, but it didn't match its predecessor's success, making it into the playoffs just once in three seasons before disbanding.

Hockey at its highest level arrived in Phoenix in 1996. To the members of the Winnipeg Jets, it might have felt like a lesser sun-drenched exile than it had to Howie Young before them. With a small market and a soft Canadian dollar, the Jets weren't financially viable, and their ownership, tired of the red ink, dumped the fran-chise to Phoenix businessmen Steven Gluckstern and Richard Burke, who bought into Commissioner Gary Bettman's much-derided strat-egy of growing the game in the Sun Belt as a means to getting a U.S. network television deal. Ownership decided that the Roadrunners' name didn't pack much weight in the market and might only confuse people who knew of them as a minor-league team. The franchise was rebranded the Coyotes, but they weren't quite a howling success in their first seasons.

Understand that Phoenix Coyotes hockey, in its early days, had a sideshow aspect. America West Arena, the team's original home, couldn't really accommodate hockey—the floor had to be retrofitted for a two-hundred-foot ice surface, so the upper bowl actually hung over the ice. Up in the cheap seats, the view of the games wasn't obstructed so much as it was halved. Spectators in the front rows could see maybe three-quarters of the sheet, and in the absence of a jumbotron, they would have to take it as an article of faith that a goal was scored or a save made.

In a mostly unsuccessful attempt to sell tickets to entry-level hockey fans, the Coyotes tried to turn games into family events where the game itself played out in the background. The day that I saw the Senators face the Coyotes, a mariachi band played by the snack bar, and the team mascot cavorted with the kids while parents hit the beer stand.

That was the scene at America West Arena just after Matthews celebrated his first birthday. His parents, Brian and Ema, had moved from Northern California to Phoenix just weeks before. The idea that an NHL star would come from Phoenix as a by-product of the Coyotes would have seemed as remote as Alpha Centauri. Further away still was the idea that a star on the ice would have been born to a father who hadn't even seen two-thirds of an NHL game and a mother who, growing up in Hermosillo, Mexico, barely knew a thing about hockey at all.

Matthews was three when he attended his first NHL game, watching from his uncle's season-ticket seats. Exactly what made a big impression on the boy is lost in the fog.

"I remember it being really loud," Matthews said in a *New York Times* interview. His mother remembers it a different way: "I think it was the Zamboni coming out on the ice between periods that was exciting for him." Soon he wanted to go to games more frequently, and his interest in the game went beyond the acoustics and ice maintenance.

Matthews's interest in the game would probably have been no different if it had been any of the iterations of the Roadrunners playing in the arena rather than the NHL. The nuance of the game would have been lost on a preschooler. Then again, no professional hockey star with Arizona roots had come along during the Roadrunners' time. Prior to Matthews, the single NHL player born in Arizona was Philadelphia's Sean Couturier, an NHL first-round draft pick whose New Brunswick–born father had coached Phoenix's minor-league team in the early 1990s, just another whistle-stop for a hockey lifer. The younger Couturier stayed in the Sun Belt only so long as his father coached the Roadrunners.

Brian Matthews did know a thing or two about sports, however. He had played baseball as a young man. And elite sports ran deeper in Matthews's extended family. Wes Matthews, Auston's great-uncle, played college football at a small state school in Oklahoma, and, as an undrafted free agent wide receiver, was permitted a one-year deferment from the Vietnam War to play a season for the Miami Dolphins. In his own way, Wes Matthews had come out of nowhere, and his message to Auston was simple: Strip away pedigree and everything else. "It's mano a mano; you against the other guy," he said.

Given the Matthews family's history and the sports landscape in Arizona, it seemed likely that Auston would become a ballplayer of some sort. High school sports in Arizona focus on the big three: football, basketball, and baseball. Every school has a gym, a court, and a diamond, and the city and state championships play out in a big way in the pages of the sports section and on sportscasts. Baseball is probably the biggest going concern, closest to the game of worship—among the children in Matthews's middle-class neighbourhood, baseball was easily the most popular activity. The Matthews family lived not so far from Big League Dreams sports park, which features replicas of Wrigley Field, Fenway Park, and Yankee Stadium. Hockey had little to no market share by comparison. Other than the Coyotes' arena and their practice facility, there weren't a dozen ice pads around Phoenix where a kid could skate. Given the scarcity, the hourly rate was pricey.

Auston started out playing both hockey and baseball. His parents still have the video of their son's first lap of the ice. "He had a very big grin on his face," Brian Matthews told the *New York Times* in 2015. "I remember seeing that smile and thinking, 'Dang, this is going to be an expensive sport.'"

Brian Matthews won't admit to pulling for his son to stick with baseball, but it's easy to imagine. He also understands why Auston, at age six, ended up telling his dad that he wanted more than anything to play hockey.

"I think he loved baseball," said Brian. "But there was too much standing around for him. If he could have batted every fifteen seconds, he would have loved it. Waiting around for the pitcher to throw the ball, it wasn't active enough for him."

For her part, Ema says she didn't feel like she could or should point her son in one direction or the other. "I didn't know anything about sports. In Mexico, as a girl, you weren't supposed to play sports. I knew about soccer and I knew some about baseball—Brian played when he was young, that I knew. I knew nothing about hockey, but I was going to do what I could to help out. I could see that he was gifted in whatever he took up. He would get so serious about anything that way. Pretty soon after he told us that he wanted to play hockey, our whole life changed. Whatever it was going to cost and whatever we'd have to do, we were going to do it."

Brian and Ema will joke that they didn't see any point in taking

Auston to an orthodontist because they figured they'd be investing in dental work that would be a casualty of the game he loved.

After Matthews's four-goal outburst, the pro scouts packed up and left the Ottawa arena with their notebooks and first impressions. "They've got some incredibly skilled kids in Matthews and Nylander, though Marner didn't really do anything to stand out," the one scout said. "I liked what the other kids did. That Hyman kid plays hard down low, on the wall, and he's smart—he shouldn't be a top-six forward or anything, but he can help a team if he's a third- or fourth-liner. You can win with him, and the same with Brown. Even the Russian on blueline looked like he has some game."

At TKO's, the patrons tried to tamp down wild enthusiasm and shape it into cautious optimism, to be expected of those who had been burned so often and so severely. "If Matthews can stay healthy," Dave Pal said, "if they can find someone to play with him . . . Remember those years [Mats] Sundin had nobody to pass to, Jonas Hoglund, Chad Kilger . . . Honestly, I think this team is really going to struggle. But I'm fine with that. I'm fine if they tank and play for another top-three pick. They're not a playoff club, not all the kids in this line-up. This isn't their year. I dunno. Tonight the stars lined up and we got a look at the future."

The impact of Matthews's four-goal night was felt far beyond the arena in Ottawa and the city limits of Toronto. The Leafs–Senators game was being watched intently all around the hockey world by many who felt deeply connected to Matthews, many whose hearts beat a little faster each time the red light flashed.

A Ukraine-born hockey coach was sitting in his living room in Scottsdale, Arizona, and explaining to his young son that it was the same Auston that they saw at the rink during the summer and "he won't score four every night."

In Madison, Wisconsin, another coach, a hockey lifer born into a hockey family, held his iPhone, which was pinging nonstop. "Incredible, so proud," he typed as he wiped away a tear.

In Zurich, Switzerland, in the dead of night, a thirty-two-year-old pro in his last season closed his laptop after the game. Only later would he be able to articulate his thoughts: "It's like I saw all that before. It's winding down for me, but as long as Auston's going to play, it's like a bit of me is out there. And he's going to play a long time."

CHAPTER TWO

THOSE WHO HAD ANY LIVING MEMORY OF THE LEAFS' LAST
Stanley Cup victory would, by the time Auston Matthews was suiting up, have to be around retirement age. I was nine back in the spring of 1967 and remember having been sent to bed when Game 5 against the Canadiens went into double overtime—I cracked open my bedroom door so I had a view of the black-and-white set in the distance and watched Bob Pulford score the winning goal while I stood in my pajamas. I imagine that only a handful of fans who were in attendance at Maple Leaf Gardens that night are still going strong, but then again, a surprising number of players from that Leafs team are still with us half a century later—septuagenarians, octogenarians, and, in the case of Johnny Bower and Red Kelly, even nonagenarians. Only seven who played for the Leafs that year have passed away.

The vast majority of fans know of that team only from the vintage footage, from the grainy clip of the goal that clinched the Cup, George Armstrong putting the puck in the net after the Canadiens had pulled Gump Worsley in Game 6. They've seen still photos from that game. They've heard the names over and over, likewise the stories chapter and verse.

The franchise hasn't made the Stanley Cup finals since, and has spent many of the intervening years in hockey's wilderness—proportionally, more fans are familiar with the Leafs' travails and shortcomings in the seasons after 1967 than they are with the win itself. Fans in their late forties or early fifties would remember the sideshow when owner Harold Ballard fired coach Roger Neilson and then, after a public and internal outcry, voided the termination—Ballard floated the idea of keeping his decision a mystery and having Neilson go out to the Leafs bench wearing a paper bag over his head for the big reveal. Ballard alienated many of his best players, including Hockey Hall of Famers Dave Keon and Darryl Sittler, who once played in a sweater with a hole over its heart after he'd cut off the captain's *C*.

Fans younger than that will remember Wendel Clark coming along in the mid-1980s. Not long into Clark's tenure, King Clancy—Ballard's most loyal and possibly only friend—died. Around that time, Ballard hired a thirty-year-old former office boy, Gord Stellick, to be the team's general manager. That, of course, didn't last. Nothing really did. The Leafs' owner became entirely unmoored just a few years later, and upon his death, the conventional wisdom was that management of the team could only get better. And it did.

Cliff Fletcher came in with a Stanley Cup ring from Calgary, where he had put together the 1989 team that had won it all. Fletcher's first moves were golden: bringing in coach Pat Burns and trading for Doug Gilmour. With those two leading the way, the team made it to the Western Conference finals in 1993 and '94. But Fletcher's veteran-laden team got old almost overnight, and he shipped out big contracts for pittances at the trading deadline in 1997. I was there when he told reporters he had turned down an offer of a first-round pick in trade for Clark and shot down their questions about his passing up the deal for a draft future. Fletcher uttered two words, a personal coinage that has lived on ever since and haunted him: "Draft, schmaft." He had long maintained that Toronto fans wouldn't tolerate a rebuilding process, that they demanded instant and constant gratification. It was, of course, just an assumption, a theory that had never been tested.

The late 1990s and early 2000s were a curious time. Two executives, polar opposites in personality, wrestled for power: the bone-dry and professorial Ken Dryden, the Hall of Fame goaltender with the Canadiens in the 1970s, and the beloved hockey lifer Pat Quinn, a former tough guy with the Leafs in the 1960s and early '70s. As GM, Dryden hired Quinn to coach the team, but, in something of a putsch, the latter squeezed out the former: Dryden wound up on the board, and Quinn coached and managed a team that was, in some senses, similar in makeup to Fletcher's veteran squad. Inevitably, Quinn himself was relieved of his GM post, which was handed to John Ferguson Jr., son of Montreal's tough guy from the 1960s. Ferguson Jr. had worked behind the scenes in the league for years and never seemed comfortable in the spotlight—for fans, he was at best a regrettable hire, but one that set the stage for the Leafs' boldest-ever management hiring to that point.

The franchise made a seismic splash in November 2008 when, just two weeks after he had stepped down as Anaheim GM, the board signed Brian Burke to a six-year contract that paid him $3 million a year, making him one of the highest-paid executives in league history. The Leafs weren't just paying for Burke's extensive CV—he had been a GM in Hartford, Vancouver, and Anaheim, where he had won a Stanley Cup in 2007—they were buying his public persona, a brusque, even confrontational old-school hockey man. In sharp contrast to Ferguson, Burke embraced the spotlight, showing up on panels on *Hockey Night in Canada* and playing to the cameras. Public confidence in the Leafs' direction was never higher than the day he was formally announced. Burke's willingness to walk away from a seemingly swell situation in Anaheim spoke to the considerable cachet the Toronto franchise, however beleaguered, still commanded.

On the day of his hiring, Burke offered a mission statement that showcased his thesaurus and attitude. What he wanted on the ice were players in his image as an executive, and it was pure red meat for Leafs Nation, or at least so Burke thought.

"We require, as a team, proper levels of pugnacity, testosterone, truculence, and belligerence. That's how our teams play," he said. "I make no apologies for that. Our teams play a North American game. We're throwbacks. It's black-and-blue hockey. It's going to be more physical hockey here than people are used to."

Burke went on at length about introducing "snarl" into the Leafs' line-up and icing a bigger team with the promotion of minor-league tough guy André Deveaux, who would record no goals, one assist, and nine fights in twenty-one games with the team. Deveaux has long been forgotten, but the bombastic "truculence" speech would be invoked ruefully over the years. It turned out to be both Burke's mission statement and a postmortem.

If Burke ever said, "Draft, schmaft," it was out of earshot of a reporter. Nonetheless, with regard to building a team, he seemed to believe, like Fletcher, that anything like rebuilding had to be done on the fly. He seemed to feel that the fans were of a mind like his own—impatient and demanding quick returns. And, like Fletcher, Burke saw draft picks as a currency that he didn't mind spending. Thus, in his first, biggest deal, he sent two first-round picks (No. 2 and No. 8 overall in successive years) and a second-rounder to Boston for Phil Kessel, a one-dimensional sniper who had worn out his welcome with the Bruins. Perhaps it was the price you would pay in trade for a franchise player; Kessel was talented, but a franchise player he was not. Nor was Dion Phaneuf, the defenceman Burke acquired in trade from Calgary. The cost in futures in that trade was minimal, but Burke's estimation of Phaneuf was outdated—he failed to pick up his game, which had declined since he was runner-up to Niklas Lidstrom in the Norris Trophy voting in his third season in the league. When Phaneuf struggled early, Burke doubled down and named him captain in an attempt to raise his game. It never seemed like a good fit.

What could go wrong did. Burke surrounded himself with his friends—Dave Nonis as assistant GM, Ron Wilson as coach. He eschewed data analytics, which were being rapidly adopted by teams around the league. He picked battles with the media. For many, he went from savior to the object of ridicule. When the Ontario Teachers' Pension Plan announced the sale of its controlling stake in Maple Leafs Sports and Entertainment (MLSE) to a consortium featuring Rogers and Bell in December 2011, the fund walked away with $1.32 billion. The unlikely corporate partners had secured a storied franchise that, under Burke's direction, was going to miss the playoffs for a fourth straight year. At the end of the NHL lockout in January 2013, the new management fired Burke.

When the deal between the league and the players' association was finalized, the orderly world of the Toronto Maple Leafs seemed to have been restored. Players were to report beginning on January 8, 2013, with full-on practices to commence the following day. The Leafs' schedule was posted on their website, a broadcast line-up was hammered out, and the few tickets that weren't allotted to season-ticket holders were snapped up. Day-to-day operations had jump-started after a four-month hiatus. And then, seemingly with no notice, everything changed at 10:30 a.m.

Sportswriters who had been heading out to the Maple Leafs' practice facility in Mimico picked up their cell phones, read messages from the team's media relations department, and then rerouted to the ACC. That morning, sports-talk radio conversations had focused on what Year 5 of Brian Burke's slow-to-unfold rebuilding plan would look like. In columns in the morning papers and in stories posted online, there was speculation about Burke's chances of swinging a trade for Vancouver goaltender Roberto Luongo, supposedly all that separated the Leafs from a deep playoff run. No one was ahead of the news—which is to say that everyone was blindsided by the word out of the Maple Leafs' offices: MLSE had fired Brian Burke.

At lunch that day, in the media room at the ACC, the company staged what was to that point the strangest press conference in the history of Toronto sports. Tom Anselmi, MLSE's executive vice president and chief operating officer, sat at the microphone and brought the proceedings to order with the bedside manner of a practiced oncologist. Sitting beside Anselmi was Dave Nonis, effectively Burke's next of kin. Anselmi stuck to the rote script in announcing that Nonis, previously the assistant general manager, was taking over for Burke, the man who had hired him twice, first in Vancouver and then with the Leafs.

"This is more about tone and the voice of leadership than changing gears and going in a different direction," Anselmi said.

By scale, the biggest change, of course, had already occurred back in August, when the Ontario Teachers' Pension Plan had been bought out. Judging by Nonis's unsmiling, even mournful demeanor, there was a tacit understanding in the upper reaches of the organization that more changes were inevitable. Some might have presumed that Nonis restrained any enthusiasm out of respect for Burke, his longtime friend. That would have put the best possible—though highly improbable—spin on it. Anselmi's unemotional delivery and flat tone told all: This wasn't Nonis's team now, but rather Nonis's *for* now. The new GM recognized that his status as best friend of yesterday's man afforded him almost no job security or time, and he hinted at the fact in his few measured words to the media.

"Once we get the green light, we're going to have a very short window to make some decisions about this hockey team," Nonis said.

Burke, Anselmi said, would stay on with the team as "a senior advisor," a coded message. Burke was going to remain on the payroll while negotiating a buyout of the remaining eighteen months on his six-year, $18 million contract. No one in hockey could imagine that Burke would settle for such a neutered role with any team, never mind one that had just punted him. Anselmi seemed almost too eager and comfortable in delivering the shocking news that effectively put everyone involved with the team on notice. It had to give some in the organization amusement if not satisfaction or relief when it turned out that Anselmi would be one of the first gone—it was less than six months before he was demoted to an advisory role and a couple more before he resigned and was boxing up his belongings in MLSE's offices.

The shock of Burke's firing still seemed to be registering the next morning when the Maple Leafs took the ice for their first workout. Teams usually invite sixty players to their camps in September—recently drafted teenagers get to work out with pros, young pros who've spent a season or two in the minors get a chance to play their way up on the organizational charts, and the veterans and stars get a few good sweats on before earning their keep in the regular season. What awaited, however, was no regular season not for the league, which would be playing a compressed forty-eight-game schedule, and definitely not for the Leafs, who had been assembled by a pink-slipped GM and who had heard all too clearly MLSE's directive for "a change in direction."

The Leafs' training facility, the former Lakeshore Arena in Mimico, didn't lend itself to any sort of theatre. But for a press box and a few more aluminum benches, it resembled any one of the dozens of neighbourhood rinks scattered around the city. It was a place where professional players went to put in the mundane work necessary to their games. Nonetheless, the pros tried to break up the routine with chatter on the ice, harmless trash talk, and a few mock cheers when anybody showed off some skill. None of that was in evidence at the first workout, however, which could have been scored with a dirge. Randy Carlyle blew whistles and barked out drills, and his voice echoed around the arena like it was a haunted house. His assistants talked to individual players in voices not much louder than whispers. Players who had spent several seasons together, who hadn't seen each other in the better part of eight months, went about the drills as though each of them were returning to work after a death in the family. There might have been some tension hanging in the cold air out on the pad, but it was clear in the aftermath that it had been trumped by dread. While players on the twenty-nine other teams around the league were talking about how excited they were to be back at the rink and the prospects for the season ahead, Carlyle and the Leafs knew they were going to have to talk about Burke's firing.

First to speak was Dion Phaneuf, in keeping with his role as team captain. For two seasons, Phaneuf had tried to fill the role as the Leafs' team leader and spokesman for the players, but it never quite came off. Those who knew Phaneuf from his Calgary days knew exactly what a poor fit he was for the captaincy, and it was never plainer than in this moment. His words were as empty as the rink that awaited the Zamboni for a flood.

"I was definitely shocked," Phaneuf said, according to the Canadian Press. "I have a lot of respect for [Burke]. But now we move forward. Like I said, I've got a good relationship with [Nonis], and now as a group, we're ready to work for him and go in the direction that he wants us to."

Phaneuf talked about coming together at a time when everything seemed bound to come apart. His confidence—the same kind shared by many players, that they can always play their way out of a bad situation—seemed to sustain him, and others would follow suit. Like Nonis at the press conference, Phaneuf talked about the immediate future, not the long term, but he did so neither confidently nor convincingly. Unlike Nonis, Phaneuf seemed incapable of imagining any scenario in which he was already part of the past.

The throng of reporters and television cameramen moved the length of the rink to the Leafs' dressing room. The media relations staff had staged Phaneuf's time with the media well—he was all on message. But the staff didn't have as much control over the rest of the players. In stark contrast to the home team's spacious country-club dressing room at the ACC, the dressing room at the Lakeshore Arena was cramped. More than that, there was no escape. The players-only area at the ACC is a warren of trainer's rooms, weight rooms, and equipment rooms through which players can duck out after security opens the doors to the media. At the Lakeshore Arena, the players had to go out the same door that the media was barging through, and the reporters made the most of it.

Joffrey Lupul had become the go-to quote in the Leafs' room since Burke had swung a deal for him and Jake Gardiner with Anaheim. Lupul didn't let the reporters down, doing exactly what Phaneuf had avoided—accepting the blame for Burke's dismissal.

"[The timing] was weird, but we haven't made the playoffs in however many years, so the blame is falling right now on the GM," he said to the *Toronto Star*. "At the end of the day, it's our responsibility. He put faith in us and we didn't get the job done last year, and now he's paying the price."

The reporters went from one Leafs veteran to another, looking for others who would echo Lupul's sentiments. All anyone wanted to talk about was Burke. If the MLSE's new proprietors hadn't made such a bold executive move on the eve of the season, one young player new to the team would likely have been the story of the day.

If Morgan Rielly felt overwhelmed by the situation, you could hardly have blamed him. Any eighteen-year-old dropped into the maelstrom would find his head swimming. This was his day one with the Leafs and day thirty-something living out of his suitcase. He had left the Moose Jaw Warriors at the start of December and joined the Canadian team for the world juniors in Ufa, Russia. The team had initially showed promise but narrowly lost its last two games after New Year's and returned home without a medal. Rielly's trip home was torturous. He had an unexpected layover in London after missing a connecting flight on the way home. Upon landing in Toronto, he found out that he wouldn't be flying on to Saskatchewan to rejoin the Warriors after all. With the NHL back in business, Rielly was to report to the Leafs camp.

Rielly asked the team's media relations staffers to recommend a hotel. He'd barely checked in and sent out dry cleaning, when he heard that the Leafs had fired Burke, the man who had called Rielly the best player in the entire draft class back in June. Rielly hadn't known exactly where he stood in the organization. Burke had sent mixed messages just days before, in one breath saying he was reluctant to rush a teenage defenceman into an NHL line-up, in the next saying that Randy Carlyle had done it before in Anaheim with Cam Fowler and that it was entirely Carlyle's call. It was little wonder that, jet-lagged and groggy, Rielly had slept through his wake-up call and missed the exit on the drive out to the Leafs' practice facility. Rielly was like an extra on the set of a soap opera, there in body but trying not to call attention to himself. Naturally, he didn't have deep thoughts about Burke's firing.

"He has always been great to me and always treated me as a pro," Rielly said. "But I guess that's how it goes sometimes. It's tough."

Rielly expressed no expectations about making the cut or playing any games with the Leafs—he had missed virtually the entire previous season with a torn anterior cruciate ligament and was just finding his form when the Canadian junior team called.

"All I can do is get out there and play my best," he said. "I think I'm lucky just to get a chance to be here."

As it turned out, Rielly would last only four days in training camp before being sent back to his billets' home in Moose Jaw. For a teenager who dreamed of playing in the NHL, it might have seemed a disappointment. But in reality, it was the best thing that could have happened. Rielly wasn't cut from the team so much as quarantined. The future of the team didn't rest with the remnants of the past. Within thirty-three months, with the exception of Rielly, most of the major figures of the past—from Phaneuf, Lupul, and Kessel through to the executives Nonis, Carlyle, and Anselmi—would be out of the organization. There was only risk in keeping Rielly around while Burke's fingerprints were wiped from the organization. There was no reward for bringing in the teenager before the rebuilding started in earnest.

The drafting of Rielly proved to be the last gasp of Burke's management, and the decision to send the teenager back to junior by Nonis and company would prove to be wiser than anyone could have known back in January 2013. It was validated by the outcome.

Just three calendar years after the lockout season, Rielly was playing a significant role in the event that set back the start of another NHL season: the 2016 World Cup of Hockey. In the weeks running up to the Leafs' opener in Ottawa, Rielly had played for Team North America, which comprised the best young Canadian and American players in the NHL.

You wouldn't have categorized Rielly as a breakout star—there were younger players who already were bigger names on the Team North America roster: Connor McDavid, Jack Eichel, and Auston

Matthews among them. Still, Rielly gained a new level of apprecia-tion during the competition. For the first time in his NHL career, he was playing meaningful games and surrounded by transcendent tal-ent. Also, for the first time as a pro, he was cast as a leader, if for no other reason than that he wasn't the kid in the room anymore but in fact the oldest and most experienced. At twenty-two, he was a vet-eran presence.

In the run-up to the World Cup, Rielly's might have seemed like just another name on the roster, filling out space. To some, his pres-ence in the line-up there signified Team North America's apparent weakness: an imbalance in the level of talent by position. The con-ventional wisdom was that Team North America's blueline was a patchwork. It was to be expected, given that most elite defencemen aren't physically mature enough at eighteen or nineteen to compete in the NHL like their counterparts up front do. But Rielly fit right in, looking like he truly belonged with the game's elite when he worked the point on Team North America's power play, quarterbacking a unit that featured McDavid, Eichel, and, yes, Matthews.

When Rielly had reported to his first pro training camp during that lockout-shortened season, and when he'd made the Leafs' ros-ter the following fall, he had arrived at the worst possible place at the worst possible time. The Leafs were about to be torn down and rebuilt. In the meantime, he had been expected to blossom in the rubble. Somehow, and to his credit, Rielly managed to come out of the team's teardown unscathed by the experience.

Mike Stothers, Rielly's coach in Moose Jaw, had his own theory about how the young defenceman got through it. The way Stothers saw it, Rielly had perspective. He was able to see the long game in Toronto, to look down the road and not get caught up in the losing. After all, Rielly had already had to adopt that attitude as a teenager when he lost a season to a torn ACL.

"I'm really not surprised by how it came together for Morgan," Stothers said. "The knee injury was a blow. It had to have been a scare to him. It would be to anybody. He could have gotten down about it, but he didn't. He never stopped being part of the team the whole time he was in recovery and rehabbing. He was at practice every day because he liked being around the other guys and in the arena—there's more to [hockey] than just the game on the ice, and, really, that was the only thing he couldn't do for all those months. And maybe because he couldn't do that, he dove into the other stuff. He never let it be about him not being in the line-up. He made it about what he was going to do when he got back on the ice. That injury didn't set him back, as it turned out. It did impact him—at least in how he looks at the game and his career."

The decision by Nonis and company to send Rielly back to Moose Jaw in January 2013 would have been entirely consistent with the philosophy of the management team that MLSE would eventually adopt down the line. Brendan Shanahan arrived during Rielly's rookie season, and, in turn, Shanahan brought in Lou Lamoriello to be the general manager. It was easy to read into the move a loyalty that stretched back almost thirty years. Back in 1987, Lamoriello, then in his first year as GM in New Jersey, used the Devils' first-round, second-overall pick to select Shanahan. Later, when Shanahan, past the age of forty, was looking to play one last season, he signed with the Devils again.

Coming out of his draft year, Shanahan jumped straight from the London Knights into the Devils' line-up at age eighteen, but he was the exception in Lamoriello's long tenure in New Jersey. Lou's management philosophy when it came to young players was simple: Better to bring them in a year late than a year too early. An elite prospect, in his teens or barely out of them, can lose his compass. Making the grade is incredibly difficult even in ideal circumstances in the NHL—even those set up to win can still fail.

The circumstances in the 2015–16 season, the tank year, had been the farthest thing from ideal—tough enough for a player like Rielly, who had a couple of seasons of experience, to survive, and too challenging by half for an eighteen-year-old, no matter how gifted. Just one day after Matthews's four-goal explosion against Ottawa, then, the question at the front of everyone's minds was clear: Were the young Leafs ready?

CHAPTER THREE

THE CROWD AT THE ACC ON THE OPENING SATURDAY NIGHT OF
the season was still buzzing forty-eight hours after Matthews's four-goal debut in Ottawa. Leafs fans hardly needed any prompting, but *Hockey Night in Canada* went all in with its introduction for the broadcast of Toronto's opener against the Bruins. The producers would hardly need an excuse to invoke history at the top of the show, but the league's centennial season gave them license to pull out the stops. The grainy black-and-white footage of Foster Hewitt and the game back in the 1940s and '50s with Maurice "Rocket" Richard, Jean Béliveau, and Gordie Howe gave way to highlights from the modern era: Bobby Orr, Wayne Gretzky, and Mario Lemieux, followed by contemporary stars Sidney Crosby, Alexander Ovechkin, and Jonathan Toews. The last to skate across the screen was the next generation of hockey genius, Connor McDavid, and then, yes, Auston Matthews. With less than two days to work with, the producers had managed to insert not only Matthews's spectacular second goal against the Senators but also the shock and wonder on his mother's face. And in no way did it feel like unnecessary hype. McDavid missed more than thirty games of his rookie season but erased any reasonable doubt that his talent was sine qua non—despite his limited body of work, there was a consensus among scouts not only that McDavid was the fastest skater in the league but also that he was probably one of the fastest going right back to Foster Hewitt's day.

Matthews had played only a bit more than sixty minutes in the NHL, but to the satisfaction of those same scouts, any ambition he had to someday take his place beside the legends seemed justified.

In the arena before the start of the broadcast, Leafs management was looking after the franchise's too-often-neglected history. It had long been a quirk of the team not to retire the numbers of its greatest players. With all their Stanley Cup winners over the years, the Montreal Canadiens had retired a long list of numbers—3, 6, and 8 were the only single digits available. The Leafs, on the other hand, simply "honoured" players with banners with their name and likeness hanging from the rafters. Going back to the darkest days of Harold Ballard's ownership in the 1970s and '80s, there wasn't even that. For the cantankerous and utterly unsentimental Ballard, it would have been like the Granite Club putting up plaques to honour waiters, groundskeepers, and janitors. MLSE's plan was to fix this oversight in a night. All those honoured players would have their numbers officially retired. The living stars were flown in and introduced to the crowd—*Armstrong, Keon, Salming, Sittler*—as were the families of the departed—*Apps, Broda, Kennedy, Horton*. In the Leafs' dressing room, James van Riemsdyk was wearing a never-worn sweater with his new number, 25, while his old number, Börje Salming's 21, was raised and the ACC crowd gave the colourful Swede a standing ovation. Fans of a certain age might have entertained thoughts that, years down the line, they could be in the arena as Matthews's 34 was retired. The more clear-eyed believers would recognize that as a fanciful idea, given that even the likes of Orr and Gretzky wound up playing for more than one team, and that Keon and Sittler had left Toronto in unpleasant circumstances.

Though the season was just entering its first weekend, the midweek openers had provided no shortage of drama. Matthews was the biggest story in the earliest news cycle, to be sure, but far from the only one. McDavid picked up a couple of goals and an assist in Edmonton's 7–4 win over Calgary in the Oilers' home opener. And Boston's Brad Marchand, who had gone from garden-variety pest to a linemate of Crosby during the World Cup, racked up two goals and three assists in the Bruins' win in Columbus.

The Bruins figured to be a useful measure of the young Maple Leafs. Boston still had a lot of key pieces in place from the Stanley Cup winners back in 2011, including towering defenceman Zdeno Chara and Patrice Bergeron, the centre who fills opponents' elite scorers with dread. But five years later, more than a few of the frontline players from that championship team had moved on, and Chara had turned forty. Boston was in transition, if not full rebuild mode like the Leafs. The Bruins had finished 24 points ahead of the Leafs the year before, but they'd missed the playoffs by the barest of margins—a tiebreak. They were seemingly going to have to make the playoffs to save the job of Claude Julien, who had coached the team to its last Stanley Cup but had since lost the confidence of management.

For the Leafs, though, the story coming out of Game 2 of the season was Mitch Marner. It remained unclear whether Toronto's front office and coaches had much confidence in him. The Leafs weren't publicly tipping their hand about their plans. Back in the spring, Lou Lamoriello was as coy as ever. Mike Babcock told reporters that any chance of Marner making the team would ride on the work that he put in over the summer. In marked contrast to Matthews, who expressed confidence in his ability to become a franchise centre in the mold of Anze Kopitar and Toews, the nineteen-year-old Marner was uncertain what his season would look like. Looking back on that time, Marner would say months later, "I came in hoping just to make the team, not knowing if I would [or] what type of role they had in mind for me. Really, it was nothing more than that."

Back in Marner's first NHL training camp, the Leafs seemed to have little choice but to send him back to the London Knights of the Ontario Hockey League. They couldn't justify having any first-rounder around for the duration of the tank season, never mind a winger who might have weighed only 160 well-stretched pounds on a five-eleven frame. It didn't seem judicious or even humane to put a kid in harm's way. A year later, Marner's body of work top to bottom was as impressive as any player to come out of major junior—he won the CHL's player of the year and was the driving force on a Knights team that steamrolled everyone in its way en route to the Memorial Cup championship. There seemed little benefit in sending him back again, and yet there he was, still just a few pounds heavier and so young looking that he could pass for a ringer at a midget tournament. It was the NHL or junior, though, no middle ground. Because William Nylander and Kasperi Kapanen had been drafted into the NHL from European-league teams, they'd had a chance to put in time with the Marlies in the AHL. That approach to development was off the table for Marner, however, due to an agreement between the CHL and the NHL—eighteen- and nineteen-year-old NHL draftees, junior-aged, could not play in the AHL.

Given Matthews's heroics in the opening game, it was easy to miss Marner's play. You could make an authoritative call on Matthews, but not on Marner—it would have been too early to say that he was ready to stick with the big club. He seemed to work on the periphery of the action, rather than in what coaches will call the "dirty areas": the slot, the front of the net, and other areas on the ice where a player is likeliest to get leaned on or bumped or worse. "I still had to show what I could do," Marner would say later.

The night of Toronto's home opener, Marner came out of the Leafs' dressing room on the walk to the gate, one step behind Matthews and one ahead of Morgan Rielly. If he was confident that he was going to make a big impression in his debut in front of his hometown fans, you couldn't have told it by the blank expression on his face and the mouthguard he gnawed on.

Though there's no playing deaf to Toronto fans, Shanahan, Lamoriello, and their team made it plain that they would do what they considered best rather than try to please fans. After Matthews's performance in Ottawa, the fans were desperate for him to take the opening face-off against the Bruins, effectively a curtain call. Babcock might be overdramatic at some turns, but he's no dramatist—and, more to the point, the organization was going to be ever mindful that Matthews's development might not best be served by star treatment. And, of course, with Babcock, line matching takes priority over all. Thus did Kadri, along with Komarov and Brown, open the game.

Though it was Brown who gave the Leafs an early lead, by the midway mark of the first period you had a sense that, just as Game 1 had been Matthews's, Game 2 was going to be Marner's. The sequence was a two-hundred-foot lightning strike. Zaitsev started the play deep in the Toronto end with a breakout pass to centre Tyler Bozak; Bozak neatly deflected the puck up the middle and found Marner cutting from the right side of the ice to the left through a soft spot in the neutral zone. The puck was a full stick length behind Marner, and he had to reach back to deflect it with a single touch up onto his forehand, a high-end piece of skill by itself. From there, Marner made his first NHL goal all on his own. He had shaken a backchecking Riley Nash, but Bruins defenceman Brandon Carlo had Marner in what looked like a one-on-one lockup position—at least until Marner pushed wide with speed and Carlo gave ground, trying to keep up. Marner hit the circle untouched, and from the dot wired a wrist shot a foot off the ice to the far side—Boston goaltender Anton Khudobin had misplayed the angle but didn't even move on the shot.

It was a goal perhaps slightly less extraordinary than Matthews's highlight-reel number in Ottawa, but it was still an auspicious one, not just for Marner but for the team. League statisticians determined that, for the first time since NHL expansion in 1967, rookies had combined to score the first six goals of a team's season. In fact, on the very next shift, William Nylander almost made it seven straight for first-year players. The string was broken by a van Riemsdyk goal later in the first period, and Milan Michalek added insurance later in the game, but in the wake of the 4–1 Leaf win, the talk was about Mitch Marner. Well, that and his mother, Bonnie.

There are no private moments of celebration left in professional sport. Television cameramen always have the placements of family members sorted out in advance of the game—not for nothing do they always sit on the side of an arena facing the cameras, never having to make do with side angles or the backs of their heads. Families are part of the drama, or, in the case of the Marners, the comedy.

When cameras cut away from Marner's celebration on the ice to show his parents in the stands, his father, Paul, was sitting beside an empty seat. Seconds later, Paul Marner was talking demonstrably on his cell phone. It was a curious sequence that was explained only a few minutes later: Moments before her son scored the biggest goal of his life, Bonnie Marner had left her seat to make a trip to the washroom. She missed seeing it live and explained the moment afterwards on *Hockey Night in Canada*: "I was washing my hands and I heard all the celebration, and then I heard 'number 16' and I said, 'Oh my gosh, that's Mitch.' So I ran over to that entrance and I'm like, 'Who got the goal?' and they go 'Marner,' and I go 'I'm his mom!' and they go, 'No you're not,' and I go, 'I *am*!' and I showed them my phone and I celebrated down there with them."

As great as the goal was, it was hardly Mitch Marner's only strong play of the game. In fact, when the coaching staff was breaking down video after the game, they would likely come back to other moments. Marner managed to draw two minor penalties: early in the first, a high stick from Marchand that was pretty much par for the Boston pest's course, and a tripping call on David Krejci, who was just one of the Bruins chasing Marner and left dangling under pressure in the Boston end midway through the second period. And at least a couple of other times Marner had the Bruins scrambling, and a ref could have raised an arm and reached for a whistle. What Babcock had to like most, however, was a defensive sequence midway through the second period. The Bruins were rallying, and the Marner–Bozak–van Riemsdyk line had been hemmed in the Leafs' end for the better part of a minute. Marner made a nice breakup of a pass back to the point to clear the zone and get a needed change.

Though it was a mature performance across sixty minutes for Marner, he immediately reverted to pure teenager state when he stepped off the ice. In the Leafs' dressing room, he was told about his mother being in the bathroom when he scored his first NHL goal. "That's awesome," he said on *Hockey Night in Canada*. "That's going to be something I can definitely talk to my mom about and give it to her."

To those who know the Marners, it was easy to imagine Mitch ripping his mother good-naturedly, of course. "Mitch is a real cutup, a wise guy who loves getting in his shots on and off the ice," said one friend. "Something like his mom missing his first goal, that's a gift that keeps on giving. He'll get a lot of mileage out of that. Fact is, though, as a family, they're incredibly close—closer than most. When Mitch put his parents' and brother's initials on his stall in the dressing room when he was playing junior, that was a genuine thing. That's how he feels about them . . . what his family means to him."

. . .

Steve Mercer, Mitch Marner's coach with the Don Mills Flyers minor-midget program, described Marner as "pretty representative of the top players coming out of the GTHL." The GTHL is the Greater Toronto Hockey League, which describes itself on its website as "the largest amateur hockey league in the world, with over 40,000 participants registered annually." According to the website, 556 teams ranging from A through to AAA levels compete, but it is almost exclusively the ninety-plus teams in AAA that produce NHL talents. The list of the GTHL's distinguished alumni on its website dates back more than one hundred years. The first two names listed are the Conacher brothers: Lionel, who was named Canada's greatest athlete of its first fifty years, and Charlie, who led the NHL in scoring back in 1935 and '36, the last Maple Leaf to hold that distinction. In minor hockey, players are listed by their birth years. Thus on the GTHL website, the Conachers are listed as 1900 and 1909, respectively. Hundreds have gone on from the GTHL to make it in the NHL, including three members of the Leafs' last Cup winners in 1967—Red Kelly, Bob Pulford, and Frank Mahovlich—and the team's current president, Brendan Shanahan. Marner's name is one of the last entries. The other two from the class of 1997 are Connor McDavid and Dylan Strome. Thus did the GTHL claim three of the top four prospects in the 2015 NHL draft. But, as Steve Mercer notes, the GTHL that produced Marner and that class is a very different league today than it was twenty years ago. "It's a whole other game, with the stakes a lot higher," Mercer said. "It's like a lot of things in the city, I guess. What started out as something else has been turned into a big business."

Mitch Marner's hockey journey didn't begin in Toronto at all, but rather about an hour to the east on Highway 401, in Bowmanville. The Marners' older son, Chris, was already playing AAA in Lindsay when they signed Mitch, age six, to play with the Central Ontario Wolves, with and against players two years older. By the time Mitch was playing in his first organized league in grade one, the arena passed for his playground.

Mitch and Chris's dad, Paul Marner, had played some minor hockey, but nothing remotely close to Triple A. To his credit, he didn't try to teach the game to his sons but trusted the work to professionals. He reached out to Rob Desveaux, the head instructor at the 3 Zone hockey school in Ajax. Desveaux, a former European pro who founded the school in the late 1980s, listened to Paul Marner and told him that both of the boys were welcome to come out for skating and skill lessons—but then he caught a look at Mitch. "He was so small that I didn't even see that he was standing there beside his father," Desveaux says. "I told him, 'Look, I don't teach four-year-olds. I don't run a day care.' Paul just asked if I'd give it a try, and I gave in. I really didn't think it would work out. That first session, Paul picked up Mitch and lifted him over the boards, then put him down on the ice. But about five minutes later, Mitch was skating around, showing these puck skills like no kid I had ever seen even close to that age. There was no question that he was going to be able to keep up."

The Marner boys came out for up to three private on-ice sessions a week, and they also enrolled in camps over school holidays where they skated with groups of other kids, many of them older. The holiday campers were split into two groups, one skating in a three-hour session in the morning, the other in the afternoon. Mitch was the only kid that Desveaux let skate in both. "He was really the only one who could keep up across six hours," he said.

Mitch's age made for some strange scenes. A few times the Marners would arrive at the arena for an after-school workout with Mitch fast asleep in his equipment, Paul carrying him on his shoulder. In Desveaux's estimation, Chris Marner was a talented youngster with potential, but it was clear right away that he didn't have the same level of desire that his little brother did.

———

Desveaux gave the Marner boys the technical grounding to be elite minor-hockey players, but there was a fair bit of nurturing away from the arena. Paul and his boys would watch NHL broadcasts every night they weren't at the rink. That was a habit that started before Mitch ever laced on skates, mind you—even before his first steps. Before he was a year old, he would sit in his father's lap and stare at the screen, "mesmerized," his father would say years later. When Mitch was finally able to walk, he had a tiny stick in his hand to lean on. Soon it was road hockey and pond hockey, the benefit of living in Bowmanville. Paul would get on the ice with Mitch and show him a few rudimentary points of the game, but his son picked up a lot of it on his own. That a tiny kid of three or four would even think to go top corner was one thing; occasionally banging it off the crossbar or shooting it over the net was another. When Paul Marner told people about his son's love of the game, they had no reason to doubt him. Still, he ran into more than a few skeptics. Like virtually any other field of youthful endeavor, minor hockey is rife with parents who think their kids are exceptional, who imagine that they possess genius and are bound for great things. Paul Marner would tell people that his son was "different," that he had "a gift." Some wrote off a father who talked about his son's motor skills before the kid had enrolled in kindergarten.

And yet those same people would have had to reassess any doubts when they finally saw Mitch skating with the Central Ontario Wolves in Lindsay. At six, playing against kids who were two years older than him, and by about a head the smallest player on the ice, Mitch scored around 100 points in his first season of organized hockey. The next year, Paul switched Mitch over to a team in Clarington, where, playing up once more, now against players a year older, he racked up 180 points with the AAA novice team.

Despite Mitch's domination of that level of hockey, the local league administrators told the Marners that their son couldn't move up a level the next season. Sometimes those who oversee such leagues make such rulings out of spite and envy—that's what Wayne Gretzky was up against in Brantford back in the 1970s, and his family wound up shipping him to Toronto to play for the then-MTHL Young Nats. Still, you have to give the officials in Clarington the benefit of the doubt—they likely had legitimate concerns about Mitch's getting hurt in games against older kids, even in a noncontact league.

So, Mitch Marner moved in with his coach, Robert Desveaux, and his family in south Ajax, just off Lake Ontario, and enrolled in a local public grade school, all so that he could fulfill residence requirements to play for the Whitby Wildcats, a team that would allow him to once again "play up." The Marners would drop Mitch off at school on Monday mornings, and Desveaux would pick him up after. Desveaux would get him to the Wildcats' practices and games during the week, and then his parents would pick him up after school on Friday.

"Never once was he really homesick," said Desveaux. "He just blended in and seemed to understand that this was what he was going to have to do to play hockey . . . to get where he wanted to in the game. It's hard to imagine a kid in grade four having a sense of purpose, but Mitch actually did, in a way that some kids even ten years older haven't figured out."

The Whitby Wildcats were a good team, but they were in the Ontario Minor Hockey Association, the same loop as the teams in Clarington and Lindsay—that is to say, they weren't in the GTHL. The ultimate destination for Mitch was always the NHL, but after his time in Whitby, the Marners realized that the road to the pros went through the GTHL. This time, though, rather than Mitch finding a home to fulfill residency requirements, Paul and Bonnie moved from Bowmanville to Thornhill, just north of Toronto's city limits, so that he could play for the Vaughan Kings of the GTHL.

The Marners were hardly the first family to pack up and move for the benefit of a son's hockey career, even when the kids are in tyke and atom. In a given season in the GTHL, there are probably a dozen American kids who have moved up to Toronto, living with family members or guardians, looking to raise their games playing against the city's best. Moving from Bowmanville to Whitby and on to Thornhill was significant to Mitch Marner's development, but by no means out of the ordinary. In fact, it was there that the Marners would encounter not just the best players but also their parents, who would explore every avenue and spare no cost for their sons' betterment.

The Marners changed their address and Mitch changed teams, but there were a couple of constants.

The first was promising: Mitch continued to more than keep up with players a year older than him. Another player from north of the city was also playing up through atom and peewee—that being Connor McDavid. Marner could not only compete with McDavid but in fact could occasionally outscore him. "There might have been others who tried, but Mitch and Connor were the two under-agers who stood out and had their own rivalry going," Paul Marner says.

The second seemed potentially disqualifying, however: Mitch didn't grow—or at least he sprouted so slowly that it seemed that other players' size advantage actually increased with every step up. When he turned thirteen, he was five foot two and eighty-five pounds, and it seemed like a reckless risk to put him in a contact league against the GTHL's best, who were a year older, some already shaving. So the Marners made the decision to hold him back—that is, to have him stay in the same peewee league and to play against players his own age for the first time. It was a waiting game—bantam and minor midget are the levels in which boys turn into men.

They had to hope that there was going to be a growth spurt at some point—it wasn't like either Paul or Bonnie was short by any stretch. In fact, Paul is around six feet, and Bonnie is strikingly tall as well.

In Marner's OHL draft year, he started the season at just five feet three. Scouts admired his talent, but the general consensus was that he was just too small. "They can say that they're looking for skill, but at some level, whether they'll admit it or not, they're looking for size first," said Mercer. "I don't know how it would have played out otherwise, but Mitch was lucky that season because he started to grow. He just shot up. He must have grown five inches that year."

That growth spurt alone didn't set aside scouts' reservations—even listed at five ten, scouts thought he was too small. It's true that he was slight: he grew up but wasn't filling out at all. "He just has one of those metabolisms, no matter what he takes in, he burns it off," Mercer said.

With the Don Mills Flyers, Marner burned off pounds by the game, and he had almost none to spare. The Flyers weren't contending for a GTHL or provincial championship. They actually might have overachieved to finish fifth in the GTHL AAA minor midget, and did so largely on Marner's narrow back. In an extreme case, Mercer kept Marner on the ice for forty one minutes in one game and came up with different ploys to stall for time during stoppages to let the fifteen-year-old catch his breath and get rehydrated. Across a schedule of more than sixty league, tournament, and playoff games, Marner played as much or more hockey than any player in the GTHL. And the four and a half to five hours a week that Marner spent on the ice practicing with the Flyers were supplemented by the near-daily ice time and gym work that he put in at the Hill Academy, a private school in Vaughan that, according to its website, "provides premiere programming for next level placement and preparation . . . for dedicated student athletes."

"More than talent, I value work ethic and character with players on my teams," said Mercer. "Mitch has tons of both. I didn't have to push him to work. I had to make sure that he actually took time to rest and recover. And as far as character goes, he made everyone better. Everyone followed his lead, and he got along with everybody. He made a point of being a good teammate, treating all [of his team-mates] the same no matter what their roles."

Even when Mercer could convince Marner to take his foot off the pedal, Mitch found other ways to pour himself into the game. One seemed of a piece with the child who watched *Hockey Night in Canada* on his father's lap: video. Mitch Marner still obsessively watched NHL hockey on television, but he also watched his own games. "All along the way it seemed like he had a sixth sense of where his line-mates were, but really it wasn't just intuition or reaction," explained Mercer. "It was all that video he watched that helped him understand the game and his teammates that much better." (Most of those videos of his games in minor hockey, along with his trophies and the family pets, would be saved when a fire did $400,000 of damage to the Marner family home on his nineteenth birthday, when his parents were in London watching him in the OHL final.)

Given the OHL scouts' lukewarm interest in Marner in his minor-midget season, his family weighed options other than major-junior hockey. It seemed a good route to pursue—the conventional wisdom in minor-hockey circles is that U.S. college hockey is a good fit for young players who physically mature later than most. It would mean that, rather than going to an OHL club at sixteen, Marner would play for a Junior A team, one step below major junior. It would be a two-year holding pattern, during which, hopefully, Marner's body would catch up to his hockey skills. The University of Michigan, one of the most decorated NCAA programs, had scouted Marner, and the family had settled on the school. And that's what the Marners told OHL teams who were scouting the minor-midget ranks ahead of the 2013 league entry draft. Some who worked for OHL teams thought that the Marners' interest in Michigan was a ploy, a way to put off other teams so that the London Knights could draft him—one of the coaches who worked with Marner at the Hill Academy, Lindsay Hofford, worked as a scout for the Knights at the time.

Teams that were interested had to take the Marners at their word. Going the college route would have made sense for Mitch, especially when he was measured and weighed at the OHL's combine testing: five foot seven and a half, 130 pounds. And yet, when London's turn in the draft came around, nineteenth overall, the last pick of the first round, the Knights' GM, Mark Hunter, selected Marner, a player who was two inches shorter and twenty-five pounds lighter than the next-smallest player preceding him. Once again, it seemed, London had worked the system, but teams that complained didn't do it loudly, because Marner's selection still seemed like a reach. His growth spurt notwithstanding, there was still doubt that a player his size could have an impact in major junior. College seemed a more plausible option for Marner than it had to others looking to dissuade other organizations from selecting him.

Marner might have been the centrepiece with Don Mills, but the Knights had five high NHL draft picks among their corps of forwards, including three first-round picks from the draft the previous June: centres Bo Horvat (Vancouver) and Michael McCarron (Montreal) and forward Max Domi (Phoenix). Seventeen Knights players skated in NHL training camps the year that Marner joined the team. So Marner had no illusions about getting star treatment. Rather than playing beside one of the players who had been at NHL training camps in the fall, Marner skated on the wing of another rookie, Christian Dvorak, a seventeen-year-old from Illinois.

London is a magnet franchise for NHL scouts, simply because the Knights get many of the best players in the OHL. Scouts want to see prospects go up against tough competition, and London is the test of young talents in coming drafts. Marner made an immediate impression with one NHL scout who tracked him that season: "[Knights coach] Dale Hunter wasn't going to give Marner the keys to the place when he got there, but you could see that this kid had a high hockey IQ. He had an awareness of the entire ice surface, both ends, and he showed you flashes of skill. He came in with a lot of buzz—clearly you thought that this kid could wind up as a first-round [NHL] draft pick. He was completely unafraid of anything, as cocky as hell. He had an attitude bigger than he was." Said Paul Marner, "You have to look at Mitch's numbers and keep in mind that he wasn't getting the power-play time and ice time that the older players were."

Marner's rookie season unfolded as well as could be anticipated. He picked up his first OHL point—an assist—on a power-play goal by Kyle Platzer midway through the first period of the season opener in London, what turned out to be the winning goal in a 3–0 victory over Plymouth. He notched his first goal in the Knights' payback win over the Storm in London a couple of weeks later. The Knights' season wound up being a disappointment—as host, London was guaranteed a spot in the Memorial Cup, but the team fell in the second round of the OHL playoffs and then went winless against the champions of the three CHL leagues, scoring only four goals total in three games. Nonetheless, Marner's season had to rate as a success. His numbers were nothing like the 180 points he'd racked up in youth-league AAA play, but in his first year with the Knights, he managed to score 13 goals and 46 assists in sixty-four games, second among rookies only to Ottawa's Travis Konecny, the first overall pick in the OHL draft.

Based on that performance, Marner started showing up on NHL draft previews in the summer of 2014.

Craig Button, the former Calgary GM who earned a Stanley Cup ring scouting for the Dallas Stars in the 1990s, compiled one of the most authoritative lists for TSN. In his preseason rankings, including European skaters and all goaltenders, Button had Marner slotted No. 9, ahead of Konecny and only three slots behind centre Dylan Strome, another GTHL player who had been selected second overall in the OHL draft. Button's thumbnail profile of Marner was based on his observations rather than a polling of scouts:

> *Excellent playmaker who can make plays in and through the tightest of spaces. Very elusive with his skating but can attack & beat defenders 1–1. Sees plays unfolding and is very comfortable holding puck to allow them to develop. Plays with an assuredness that is threatening and he doesn't take a back seat in the game.*

In early summer, to the surprise of no one, Hockey Canada listed Marner among the 1997 birthdays invited to play for the national team at the Ivan Hlinka Tournament, the annual midsummer under-18 event in the Czech Republic and Slovakia. Canada wound up beating the Czechs in the gold-medal final. It seemed that the more important the game, the better Marner played. He finished the tournament with two goals and five assists in five games, including a goal and two assists in the final. All of it augured well, and Marner said all the right things in advance of his draft season. When asked about playing with his NHL draft stock on the line, in front of dozens of scouts every night, he maintained that his attitude was unchanged from his rookie trip around the league. "It feels like the same pressure," Marner told the *London Free Press* in training camp. "It's the Knights organization, and it's not a small thing to live up to. This is the fiftieth year [in franchise history], and we want to show what we've got."

What Marner didn't disclose was that he had suffered a hip pointer at the Hlinka and aggravated it in workouts over the course of training camp. He played through it, though; a creature of habit. "It's nothing to get Mitch to play," Desveaux says. "It's almost impossible to get him to take a day off or rest. He just wants to be playing—he can't sit still. I don't know if you'd label him hyperactive or anything, but that's just his nature. I honestly can't remember him ever taking a week off, or even a few days—he'd just lose it if you tried to take [the game] away from him."

Marner had made steady progress in his rookie season, never going more than a game without a point. Though his minor hockey teams didn't always win championships, he had never suffered a personal slump—if he played, he was going to score. At the start of his second season in London, his pivotal draft season, Marner slumped in an almost unthinkable way. He had one goal and five assists in ten games, far below his pace from his rookie year. When he most needed to show his stuff, there was nothing there. It was impossible to pinpoint the cause of the falloff in his production on the ice. It seemed like he was set up to take off. He was playing more than he had the previous year. He was again playing alongside Christian Dvorak, who had been drafted in the second round by Arizona the previous June but returned to London after impressing the Coyotes in training camp. If Marner's hip pointer was so troublesome, the Knights would certainly have sat him down for a stretch—the Knights were again a strong team that frequently faced outmanned opponents. Marner had claimed that he didn't feel any special pressure in his draft year, but he wouldn't have been the first touted prospect to crack under it.

Marner reached the nadir, even a breaking point, in a game against Connor McDavid, Dylan Strome, and the Erie Otters, a powerhouse team that season. With at least twenty NHL scouts in attendance, the Knights were soundly beaten 6–2, and the home team put on an absolute light show, one that starred two players ahead of Marner in the preseason draft projections. McDavid picked up a goal and two assists, and his speed drew oohs and ahs every shift. Strome was 1-and-1, giving him 30 points on the season. Marner went pointless and was a minus-2. In fact, he had gone four games without a point—he had never had a stretch like that without a goal or a multiple-point game.

At the end of the night on the major-junior circuit, players lug their sticks and equipment bags out to the team bus and throw them in the hold underneath. Parents who are able to make it out to games wait beside the bus to get a chance to talk to their sons for a few minutes. Teams are accommodating on this count—the ride home on a bus with a team that just lost might pass silently for hours at a stretch, so giving the players a chance to connect with their folks is simply a matter of respect for families who have driven hours to get to the games. Mitch Marner carried his bag out to the back of the arena but walked up to his father instead of the bus. He felt beaten, utterly lost on the ice.

"Dad, I suck," he said. "I'm so embarrassed for you and Mom. I'm no good."

As bad as he felt, he didn't want to play hockey anymore. Mitch Marner wanted to go home.

He threw his bag in the trunk of his father's car.

Paul Marner spoke to Knights coach Dale Hunter about letting Mitch come home to decompress for a couple of days. Hunter, who was at a loss as much as anyone to explain Mitch's drop-off, said he understood.

In retrospect, neither Paul Marner nor Dale Hunter believed that Mitch was walking away from the game at seventeen. No one around the Knights team or in hockey thought that a kid who had invested so much time was willing to let everything drop over a three- or four-week stretch that would be business as usual for the majority of seventeen-year-olds in major junior. That Marner wasn't up to his own standards was one thing, but it wasn't like he couldn't play at all. Mitch Marner took his ordinary play in a forgettable stretch of the fall to heart even harder than some young men would after having lost the biggest game of their lives. It seemed Mitch Marner could cope with anything on the ice except his own struggles. It's unfair to say that he had never faced adversity. The fact is, almost every shift he had ever played was against bigger and older players. He'd also been on the losing end of games. Now, though, there was a disconnect—trying harder at what had been natural to him only made things worse.

To Paul and Bonnie Marner's credit, there weren't any lectures when Mitch came home. Not a word about hockey. Not a video of the game in Erie. Not a game playing on the TV screen in the background. For the first time in years—but for a couple of times when bouts of the flu or some other malady had struck—Mitch was off skates and away from the rink.

It didn't last long. After three days, Marner told his parents that he wanted to get on the ice and skate with Desveaux. They made a call and set up a time. Desveaux was well aware of Mitch's slump, and the temptation might have been a kid-glove treatment, to tread delicately or go slow. Instead, Desveaux decided to be direct and break down the elements of the game that he had drilled into Mitch. Since the start of the Knights' training camp, a matter of two months, Mitch had fallen into a bunch of bad habits. They were plain to Desveaux in just a matter of minutes. He was shooting off the wrong foot. He wasn't prepared for passes because his stick was off the ice. Even the most basic elements of his skating were off—he was standing up too high in his stride, his crossovers were a tangle. Marner had been keenly aware of all the things he was trained to do when just in grade school, and it wasn't simply a matter of repetition on the ice—his father had videoed almost every one of Mitch's workouts with Desveaux and they had watched them together, breaking down his performance in drills. It was like a man of the cloth had somehow forgotten the Ten Commandments, all ten at once. "Mitch was relieved that there was *something* technical that we could point to and that it wasn't just one thing," Desveaux says. "He had been pretty down about how things were going. It was good just to get him smiling again."

It had never been as natural as it seemed. It had been practiced until it was habitual and unconscious. There was no way of knowing how he had strayed from everything that had made him successful. Had the hip pointer, one piece out of place, disrupted one element of his game—his skating—and then everything else fallen out of place? Or was it simply that he was pressing too hard in his draft year, what he had been building towards since his father carried him into the arena in his equipment, asleep, draped over his shoulder? Desveaux didn't want to go there. If the damage could be undone, there was no need to dive into the cause.

They skated into a second hour, and a couple of instructors from 3 Zone joined them on the ice for some drills in corner work— battling along the wall for a puck in his skates, getting his body between the puck and the defenders chasing him. At one point, Desveaux pushed Marner down to the ice. Then he did it again. And again. "That's what we had done all those years, me putting him on his ass and him getting up," Desveaux said. "And then he knocked me down. I knew he'd be okay then. It was like his competitive fire had been lit again. I said, 'Mitch, you just have to let the game be fun again. Forget the goals and the points.' The kid who wanted to go home, that wasn't Mitch. The one wanted to get back, that was him."

Marner went through a few more workouts before he headed back to London. That week, the OHL announced its line-up for two exhibition games against a touring Russian under-20 team. Despite Marner's slow start to the season, Hockey Canada and the league named him to the roster for a game in Kingston in mid-November. Though he had been on the ice with Desveaux trying to find his game just a couple of days before, Marner sounded an optimistic note when he spoke to the *London Free Press*. "It's hard to get on that team at [age seventeen]," he said. "But they gave me [a chance to play in the game], and now I've got to prove I deserve a spot and didn't get picked because of last year. Even with the year I'm having right now, they still see through that, and it means a lot to me. It's a true accomplishment to be on that team. I need to go and show I can play and it wasn't a mistake."

Back in the fold with the Knights, Marner more than justified his selection to the all-star team that was going to play the Russians. His sabbatical from the team wasn't widely advertised—if it had been, then he wouldn't have been tabbed to play in the international exhibition. He returned to the Knights in less than ideal circumstances: three games in less than seventy-two hours, home games on Friday and Saturday against Ottawa and Belleville and then a game against their rival Guelph on Sunday. In the first two games, Marner surpassed his season total in points with a goal and six assists. The next night, he scored a goal against the Storm in a rout. Over the nine games after his return from his soul- and game-searching, he rang up 27 points and was chasing down McDavid and Strome for the league scoring lead. Though he didn't pick up a point against the Russian selects in the OHL's 5–1 win, Marner wound up winning the league's Player of the Month award right after declaring himself a family embarrassment. It was like he had somehow flipped a toggle switch on his game. He was his former self and more.

In the wake of the win over Boston, Babcock didn't lavish praise on Marner or any of the other Leafs rookies. On most nights in the season ahead, he would be fine with letting the rookies' performances speak for themselves, not inclined to feel like he had to sell (let alone oversell) fans and reporters on the first-year players. On most nights, he'd talk more openly and at length about his veterans, and so it was at the end of the first Saturday night at the ACC. Babcock dwelled on the work of goaltender Frederik Andersen, who had made a few five-star saves in the second period when the Bruins were surging. That might have been strategic on Babcock's part. Even though Andersen had come over in trade from Anaheim at a significant cost (a first-round pick), and although the Leafs had given him a generous, long-term deal (five years at $5 million per year), he had yet to play in more than fifty-four games in a single season. Further, the Dane had been the presumptive number one goaltender for Team Europe at the World Cup, but a knee injury suffered in an Olympic qualifying game in the late summer had kept him out of the tournament. Andersen had been ordinary at best in the opener in Ottawa, and Babcock wanted to shut down any questions about the twenty-seven-year-old who was the franchise goaltender of both the present and the future.

Babcock spent much time at the podium talking reverentially about the legends who had their numbers retired, as if speaking for the kids in his line-up who really had no point of reference to former glories. Nonetheless, though the season was only two games old, Babcock and the rest of the hockey world had seen amazing stuff from the Leafs' rookies—not that anyone should go out and order the banners, but it would have shocked no one if you had told them that these kids would accomplish stuff and flash skills that surpassed the feats of those whose numbers were retired. They already had, and there was so much more to come.

CHAPTER FOUR

THOSE FROM OTHER PARTS OF CANADA HAVE MOCKED THE good citizens of Toronto—often with good reason—for their immense self-regard and their inability to see beyond the city limits. No one is credited with coming up with the definitive jab at Toronto—the Centre of the Universe—and thus some sharp wit squandered a million-dollar trademark opportunity. Nonetheless, on the first night of November 2016, the city was the Centre of the Hockey Universe: The Maple Leafs were hosting the Edmonton Oilers at the ACC, with the visitors' star talent, Connor McDavid, making his debut appearance as a pro in his hometown. McDavid had missed almost half of the previous season, including the Oilers' single date in Toronto, with a broken clavicle, so that November night would have been occasion enough even before Wayne Gretzky showed up in the hallways. When the reporters spotted Gretzky, they circled him and peppered him with questions about his own first game in Toronto, when the Leafs were playing out of Maple Leaf Gardens back in the fall of 1979. An event like this, Gretzky said, "is one of the great days of your life." Gretzky, who had become a partner in the Oilers' ownership group just a few weeks before, expressed high expectations—possibly proprietary—for McDavid that night: "I know he's going to be tremendously excited."

Another star, the only one in NHL history that you'd mention in the same breath as Gretzky, was also in the building that night, but he was looking to keep a lower profile. Bobby Orr, as McDavid's agent, definitely had a proprietary interest in the young Edmonton star. His attendance signified that this was a big game, but he was content to just take it in. His message was plain: This is McDavid's game now, his client's game, the player's game, not mine.

With McDavid on the ice playing in front of friends, family, and NHL legends, the night's billing as the Centre of the Hockey Universe seemed infected with Toronto hype. Or perhaps it was a push for television ratings by TSN, the, yes, Toronto-based sports network that was broadcasting the game regionally. Doubters from the rest of Canada would point to the fact that it was just November and that both the Oilers and the Leafs had missed the playoffs the previous spring by a wide margin. They'd say that any game in which Sidney Crosby and the defending Stanley Cup champions played Alexander Ovechkin and the Washington Capitals, with a decade of history between the two established superstars, was more rightfully the focus of hockey for a night.

Still, Edmonton at the ACC was more than McDavid's homecoming. The Oilers, a team that hadn't made the playoffs in more than a decade, had been one of the hottest outfits in the NHL through the first four weeks of the season, with McDavid leading the league in scoring. And the Maple Leafs, dead last in the league the previous season, had been far more interesting than what those outside the Centre of the Universe had anticipated or, probably, were comfortable with.

As all NHL players are wont to do, McDavid and Matthews played down any personal-rivalry story line going into the game. Given their personalities and their time on Team North America, it seemed genuine.

"Other than us being first overall picks in back-to-back years, that's really the only thing in common we have," said McDavid. "I know him pretty well; he's a good guy, I get along with him. I definitely don't consider him a rival. I think it would be a lot easier for you guys if I came in here and said, 'I hate him! Blah, blah, blah.' But he's a good kid. I'm excited to play against him."

"I mean, it's just another game," Matthews said. "We've got eighty-two of them this year, and we're going to play a lot of good teams, a lot of good players, so it's not like a head-to-head matchup every time you play somebody."

That's forever the players' viewpoint, but even a former player couldn't resist the story line of two young stars squaring off. "All eyes will be on those two kids," Gretzky said of McDavid and Matthews. "That's why I flew in. I'm excited to see the game. I think it's great for our sport."

The influx of youth wasn't without precedent. Three first-year players with the 1986–87 Los Angeles Kings had been named to the NHL All-Rookie team, the only time that had ever happened. Two of those three, Luc Robitaille and Rob Blake, became Hockey Hall of Famers, and the youngest among them that year, Jimmy Carson, scored 55 goals one season and remained a highly productive player across his nine-year career. Maybe you'd surmise that a bunch of young players could be dropped into the line up without much risk and to fairly good effect, but that Kings team had a bunch of veterans in their thirties, including another Hall of Famer in Marcel Dionne. Moreover, that was fully thirty years ago, when the NHL was a very different place.

Rarely in the thirty-four-year history of the All-Rookie honours have teams had a pair of their young players recognized. Just one month into the season, though, the Leafs seemed to have a lock on two, with Matthews and Marner leading the way. A third, Zaitsev— who was logging more minutes than any NHL rookie blueliner—was at the very least in the conversation. But unlike Robitaille, Blake, and

Carson, the Leafs' young stars were surrounded not by veterans but rather by other young players on the rise. Barring injury, the Leafs were going to become the first team in NHL history to play six rookies in at least seventy games.

In a way, the team that the Leafs were going to face in the Centre of the Hockey Universe was the only one that had been in a similar situation. The Edmonton Oilers were thus not just that night's opponent but also a cautionary tale. Yes, the Oilers came into Toronto cooking, but they had also been considered a basket case of a franchise, unable yet to leverage four first-overall picks and a third-overall, spread across five seasons, into a playoff berth. Five can't-miss stars, but only McDavid and his winger Leon Draisaitl, the third overall pick, had fully lived up to expectations. Two of the first-overalls—Taylor Hall and Nail Yakupov—were no longer with the team, Hall dealt in the summer to New Jersey in a deal for blueline help and Yakupov just three weeks earlier to St. Louis for pennies on the dollar. Another first-overall, Ryan Nugent-Hopkins, was still in the line-up but, in his sixth season, he didn't look at all like a first-line or even second-line centre, despite occasional flashes of skill. Edmonton painfully showed the risks involved in a rebuild, as the Oilers' fast start could be more attributed to McDavid than to the sum total of the rest of the team's prospects.

Maple Leafs fans, the Leafs Nation, were optimistic and not cautiously so, even though the team was playing just below the .500 mark and sat in second-to-last place in the Eastern Conference. Numbers mattered little—the home team was interesting again. Not only that, but there was promise that they'd be better down the line. Maybe even the playoffs next season. In two seasons' time, for sure. McDavid and the Oilers would be a measuring stick. The game was a sixty-minute window into whether the Leafs' corps of NHL novices were prompting legitimate hope or stoking irrational enthusiasm.

If the fans at the ACC got what they wanted, Toronto coach Mike Babcock would put Auston Matthews head-to-head against McDavid for the opening face-off. But that stuff happens only in the movies. Instead, Babcock matched Nazem Kadri—at twenty-six, a wizened veteran compared to the rest of the team—against McDavid.

Coming into the season, Kadri hadn't been an afterthought exactly, but many presumed that his place in the mix would be down the line. After all, Matthews and Nylander were to be the centres of the future. Was Kadri a fit as a third-line centre, usually appointed the drudgery of defensive face-offs and shadowing opponents' stars? That's not what the previous management had in mind when the Leafs drafted Kadri seventh overall in 2009. That's not what any team has in mind drafting a player in the top ten. Not that Kadri was a bust—it was just that his progress had come in fits and starts. He had spent his first two professional seasons splitting time between the big club and the Marlies, the team's AHL affiliate. When up with the big club, he had little impact with the puck and was a glaring liability without it. He seemed to take adversity hard, and his work ethic and conditioning were called into question. Fans pointed to him as just another Leafs draft pick gone bad. But even when Kadri had been deep in a snakebitten scoring slump in Babcock's first season with the club, the coach had defended him, and now Kadri was earning his keep.

From the game's opening shift, you had a sense that it wasn't going to be Connor McDavid's night—it was going to be Nazem Kadri's.

Kadri, whose game had a sneaky physical edge when he was right, dropped McDavid beside the Leafs' net on the opening shift, and thereafter it was on between them. Just seconds later, Kadri really got his adrenaline flowing when he beat Edmonton goaltender Cam Talbot to open the scoring. Kadri's right-winger Connor Brown stole the puck from Oilers defenceman Oscar Klefbom and threaded the puck through Klefbom's skates and traffic in front of the net, right onto Kadri's waiting stick. With the whole side of the net wide open, Kadri snapped the puck home to give the Leafs an early lead.

Kadri stayed in McDavid's shadow the rest of the night. Behind the play, Kadri would poke, jab, and trash-talk McDavid, and it seemed to get the young star off his game. As McDavid tired of Kadri's incessant coverage, Milan Lucic did what he was signed as a free agent to do—namely, try to scare anyone who took liberties with the franchise player. But Lucic didn't seem to throw Kadri off at all. It didn't seem to scare off anyone else in the Leafs' line-up, either—at one point in a scrum after a whistle, defenceman Martin Marincin locked up McDavid in a sleeper hold behind the Leafs' net, and McDavid couldn't break free without the officials stepping in.

The Leafs' emerging young stars, Matthews, Marner, and Nylander, had their moments and generated chances. Nylander made a slick centring pass to Matthews from behind the Edmonton net that forced Talbot to make a five-star save early. Marner danced around with the puck in the Oilers' end shift after shift—the visitors gave chase in vain, except for one shift midway through the second period when Darnell Nurse, a six-foot-four, 220-pound defenceman, laid a crushing but clean open-ice check on Marner that had the rookie and the sellout crowd gasping. The only rookie who figured in the scoring, though, was Nikita Soshnikov, who had been called up by the Leafs from the Marlies only hours before the game. Soshnikov infuriated the Oilers with elbows and slashes at every turn, and in the second period, he forced a turnover and made a slick pass to Ben Smith to give the Leafs a 2–1 lead.

Despite the young team's efforts, though, their inexperience showed, and the lead didn't stand up. Nurse tied the game with less than five minutes to go in regulation with a shot from the point that Toronto netminder Frederik Andersen muffed. The air was immediately sucked out of the building as fans reacted to what seemed like a familiar refrain—a late collapse that turned a near-victory into a bitter loss. It seemed the stage was set for McDavid's heroics to lead the Oilers to victory. But the end would be just as it was in the beginning: Kadri's moment.

Skating three-on-three at the face-off to open overtime, Kadri beat McDavid on the draw, got behind him in the neutral zone, and fought through a check at the Oilers' blueline. Carrying the puck on his backhand, Kadri flew down the right wing with McDavid on his back the entire way. Cutting across the top of the crease at the last second, he slid the puck to his forehand and tucked it around Talbot's outstretched leg for the game winner before crashing into the end boards. While the Leafs poured off the bench and mobbed Kadri, McDavid skated over to the referees and complained that he had been held on the play. McDavid didn't hide his grievance after the game, but in the Leafs' dressing room, it was unrestrained joy.

Matthews wrote a postscript on the narrative that hyperbolically positioned the game as a Battle of the Number Ones. "We were obviously very aware when [McDavid] was out there," Matthews said in the dressing room. "A lot of credit goes to [Kadri] and his line, who did a great job limiting their chances and making it hard on them."

The game had taken only a few ticks over sixty minutes, but it seemed to capture the ups and downs of the Leafs' recent history—the promise of success, the despair of victory slipping through the team's hands, the relief when they pulled things back from the brink. As the Leafs celebrated in the dressing room, you had an idea that Toronto might be the Centre of the Hockey Universe a few more times before the season was done.

• • •

Though the Oilers were in the rearview mirror for now, they would remain in the front of mind for many. The Oilers represented where the Leafs wanted to be—a little further along in the rebuilding process. Watching the Leafs skate through drills in practice at the MasterCard Centre in Etobicoke the day after the win over Edmonton, you had to wonder what changes were in the offing. For both Cup contenders and the dregs alike, players shuffle in and out over the course of a season. That season, from the run-up to the draft through to November, forty-nine players around the league had been traded, and the market hadn't even started to heat up yet—the trade deadline was still three months away.

No doubt a few of the players on the ice skating under Mike Babcock's direction in November would be listening to another coach's voice before the season was out, and more still from one season to the next. Milan Michalek, a onetime 35-goal scorer in Ottawa, had started the season with the team but was quickly sent packing to the Marlies. The most likely candidates still with the club were the Black Aces, the players who were healthy scratches the night before: forwards Peter Holland and defenceman Frankie Corrado.

At one time, not so long ago, Holland had been considered a building block in Anaheim—the Ducks had drafted him fifteenth overall in 2009. Yet his elite game as a junior had never translated to the pros. He was only twenty-two in November 2013, maybe still an emerging player, when Anaheim packed him off to his hometown Leafs in what can only be termed a minor deal (for a low draft pick and Jesse Blacker, who'd play in one NHL game before packing up to play in Germany). Holland put in two full seasons with the Leafs, including the excruciating tank season, as well as overtime with the team's training staff in the off-season.

"I felt I worked hard in the summer," he told the *Toronto Star* in training camp. "I felt like it made me a better player." It's easy to imagine that he'd be disenchanted with his reward for sticking it out: a seat in the press box most nights. Holland eventually went to Lou Lamoriello asking for a chance to play or a trade; in just two months, he'd be packed off to Arizona for a conditional draft pick down the line.

While Holland didn't hide his disappointment with the Leafs, Frankie Corrado went public with it, a little too freely for the team's liking. Corrado's frustration was understandable—he had yet to dress for a game since the Leafs had picked him up off the waiver wire in 2015. Compounding that was the fact that he seemed to fill the team's crying need for a right-handed shot on the blueline.

"How much longer are you going to be able to [stay in the league] if you don't establish yourself as a player who can keep playing in this league?" he told Terry Koshan of the *Toronto Sun*.

An affable native of Woodbridge, Corrado didn't seem to have any idea of exactly what he had stepped into. In New Jersey, Lamoriello had a record of zero tolerance for dissent, and even something as benign as Corrado's soul-searching didn't go over well with management. Babcock had no interest in discussing Corrado's (seemingly nonexistent) role with the team—a running joke among fans was that he had played as many games as Joffrey Lupul, who was on long-term disability and effectively exiled, unseen around the team all season. Bloggers formed a "Free Corrado" campaign, but it would be months before the Leafs would mercifully give him a chance at a fresh start elsewhere.

There were others in trouble as well, foremost among them Jhonas Enroth, who had struggled in his role as Andersen's backup. No. 2 goalies are considered the NHL's most interchangeable pieces, and Enroth's save percentage crested at .890—not good enough to stick in the league with an also-ran, never mind with a team that dared to imagine making a playoff run. Enroth knew he was on the clock, an impossible spot for a player in the most nerve-testing position.

The disappearances of Holland, Corrado, and Enroth and the seeming exile of Lupul couldn't have been lost on anyone in the Leafs' dressing room. Contracts might be guaranteed, but chances to play aren't. A player's position with an organization is fluid and can turn from one season to the next. Change is constant. One just has to hope that the change is for the better. And, in the case of a couple of the aforementioned, being outspoken about grievances came at a price.

CHAPTER FIVE

IT'S HARD TO IMAGINE THAT ANY NHL TEAM COMING TO PLAY AT the ACC wouldn't mark a homecoming for someone on the visiting team's roster. Likewise, games that take teams into Montreal or out west often give players an opportunity to play in front of friends. Inevitably, they'll have to field calls and texts, or scramble to accommodate those who need tickets. They'll have to hit up teammates for their comp tickets, and after the game they'll have a throng of familiar faces waiting for them by the stage door.

No analysts have ever done a deep dive on the phenomenon, but you could probably build an anecdotal case that some players shine when they play close to home. The illustrative example was none other than the league's all-time greatest scorer, Wayne Gretzky, a son of Brantford—not exactly a Torontonian, but close enough. Though he played only thirty regular-season games at Maple Leaf Gardens, Gretzky scored at a rate right around his absolute peak production whenever he played in Toronto: an astonishing 30 goals and 47 assists. It might sound ludicrous to suggest that the player who would go on to own the record book somehow played over his head when he stepped onto the ice at the Gardens, but nowhere else did he raise his game so high. It was the Leafs' good fortune that he played only thirty games there. It was also the franchise's rotten luck that they faced him in the most important game they have played in their fifty years without a Cup, Game 7 of the Western Conference finals in 1993. Gretzky picked up a hat trick in Los Angeles's 5–4 win and later called it "maybe the best game I ever played."

Maybe someday Auston Matthews will play his greatest game at Gila River Arena, what was formerly the Glendale Arena and later the Jobing.com Arena. Maybe the home of the Arizona Coyotes will be called something else. Maybe the franchise will move into another arena. In terms of magnitude of the occasion, Matthews's first NHL game in his hometown was in no way as momentous as Game 7 back in 1993. His return home was marked by a midseason tilt between two young teams, Toronto and Arizona, their best seasons at least a couple of years off, the former with wishful hopes of making the playoffs, the latter already resigned to the fact that the postseason would be out of reach. Having played for international gold medals and in the World Cup, Matthews had played for much higher stakes than he would in Glendale just before Christmas. Still, the game was special to him in a way that no one else can truly know.

This wouldn't just be Matthews's first game as a pro so close to home—it would be his first there in front of a crowd other than parents and friends. An elite kid from Toronto has a chance to play in big games on his way up—in big youth tournaments, in AAA leagues featuring future pros, in major-junior playoff games in the OHL. In the case of Connor McDavid, he had a chance to play for a world junior gold and sleep in his own bedroom the same night. Friends can track their careers on a weekly basis and even catch OHL games on TV. But Auston Matthews had always had to go away to play in the big tournaments and, in his late teens, the U.S. national programs— hockey wasn't exactly close to home in Arizona. In fact, other than viral highlight videos, there wasn't any way to watch Matthews in his earliest years unless you were in the rink. Even Brian and Ema Matthews had missed games along the way and had to travel across time zones or, as in his draft season, across the Atlantic to see their son's talent blossom. Others had to mostly rely on word of mouth about his exploits in his late teens.

Many in the Arizona youth hockey scene would have access to online services to pick up out-of-town NHL game broadcasts—no doubt Matthews's four-goal game would have driven up subscriptions. Still, many of those who would be coming out to the Gila River Arena were getting their first live eyeful of their first-ever home-grown hero. That it was scheduled over the Christmas school break gave an opportunity for players in the youth leagues to take in the game. There's no shortage of hero worship in sport in general and in the NHL in particular, but you could mount an argument that no player meant more to the grassroots of the game in his hometown than did Auston Matthews in Phoenix. So the Leafs' game against the Coyotes was a unique celebration.

"Over the last couple of years, young kids and families have been reaching out to my parents and myself when you see them at the rink," Matthews told the *Toronto Sun* the day before the game. "You want to be that person they can look up to. It's definitely a pretty big honour to be that symbol for them."

According to USA Hockey enrollment statistics for 2015, Arizona, a state with a population of more than 6.7 million, has 7,329 registered players, ranging in age from squirts and tykes through to juniors aged twenty. Not surprisingly, registration numbers in Canada dwarfed those in the American Southwest: more than 40,000 players are registered in the Greater Toronto Hockey League alone. The GTHL outstrips California (26,383) and Florida (approximately 14,000) combined. Still, there has been significant growth of the game in Arizona. In the Coyotes' first season in Phoenix, the state had 2,349 players registered with USA Hockey. By the time Auston

Matthews started going to the rink regularly, the numbers were probably up close to 4,000. Moreover, his demographic—players eight years old and younger—were the driver of that growth.

Based on that, you might presume that the game in Arizona would have been played at a rudimentary or recreational level, something along the lines of Canadian jai alai. But according to Shane Doan, a star on the Coyotes' roster from year one through to 2017, that's the furthest thing from the case.

"There were always good hockey people here as far as coaching goes, per capita maybe more than anywhere else," Doan said. "People who played the game here, whether it was in the minors way back or with the Coyotes, ended up settling here. They know the game, and when their kids wanted to play, they became involved. You had a very high level of coaching and teaching available to a pretty small or select set of kids. There weren't rinks and ice available like in other places, but there were people who knew the game. You would have someone who was qualified to coach pros teaching the game to kids who are atom age [ten] or peewee [twelve]."

That's exactly the story of Ron Filion, who had grown up in Montreal and been a diminutive but high-scoring centre in the Quebec Major Junior Hockey League. After his junior career, Filion played minor pro in France, and when he hung up his blades, he became involved with building the French national-team program. He was involved in hockey arena management in Los Angeles in 2005 when his old winger called him. Claude Lemieux, who had played on Filion's wing on the Verdun Juniors and lived with Filion's family during the season, said that he was looking to start up a hockey academy in Phoenix, where he had settled after playing three seasons with the Coyotes late in his career. Lemieux had a bigger vision than that—he would later pitch the NHL team on bringing minor-league hockey back to Phoenix, and eventually a new version of the Roadrunners

would play out of the downtown arena, this time without the mariachi band.

Filion was behind the bench for the Roadrunners' debut campaign, and finished twenty-seven games under .500. The next year,
the team showed some improvement and was tenuously holding on
to a playoff spot when, with eleven games left in the regular season,
Filion stepped down. Ready to try something else, he went back to
the grassroots—age-group hockey, right down to tyke. Among the
youngsters were Lemieux's son, Brendan, born in 1996, and Auston
Matthews. The pair "played up"—that is, skated on teams with kids
born in 1994 and 1995. Lemieux and Filion also came up with the
organization's name: the Arizona Bobcats.

The Bobcats had to struggle just to find games the first few seasons. Early on, their games were almost exclusively against teams
from around Arizona, a level that might be described as recreational. But over time, the players and their parents wanted to take
a more serious approach to the game, and they backed that up with
money. First there was a loose schedule of home-and-away games
with teams from Las Vegas and Dallas, and then, as the players grew
older, they would travel to up to ten tournaments a year in places like
Minnesota, Detroit, and Chicago. The parents followed through on
their desire to raise their sons' games with significant investments of
time and money. Matthews said his mother worked two jobs to pay
for his hockey expenses, which reached upwards of $20,000 some
years, according to his father. So much for baseball, where he could
buy his son a mitt, a bat, and a ball and take him to the sandlot.

"The key thing is coaching," said Lemieux. "Expose kids to good
coaching and they have a chance to develop, but only if they are exposed to good coaching. There was no doubt that Ron was an excellent coach—he had coached pros and knew the game. Eventually the
results were going to come."

And so they did. "When we started with the '97s, the Matthews group, we got our butt kicked everywhere we went in peewee," Filion said. "It was really tough. Two years later, we were ninth in the country."

Lemieux said that he didn't see a future NHL star in his son or Auston Matthews. He simply didn't look at the youngsters that way. "I became an agent later, working out of Toronto and other places, and I saw a lot of kids play bantam hockey, including [young stars] Connor McDavid and Max Domi. I thought that they were very good players, excellent players in that age group, but does that mean they were going to be NHLers? Not necessarily. I could see talent in Auston, sure. To be a good player in junior or some high level, okay. To be an NHL star, I don't think anyone can tell that."

Lemieux might have maintained a professional skepticism, an it's-not-true-until-you-show-me approach. Another coach who worked with Matthews, though, says that he picked up on Auston Matthews's talent and attitude from their very first skate together.

Just like in other sports, specialized skills coaches in hockey have become an industry unto themselves. Such coaches might seem scarce or absent in Arizona. But Boris Dorozhenko's unlikely, seemingly impossible route just happened to land him in Phoenix at the same time that Matthews was discovering his passion for hockey.

Dorozhenko was a Ukrainian national who grew up in the Soviet Union, playing hockey and eventually pursuing graduate studies in mathematics. His prospects at home were dim after the collapse of the Soviet Union and the resulting Ukrainian independence, and so he emigrated to Mexico—his family had connections with a formerly state-owned company that built power plants there. Dorozhenko headed up the national hockey program in Mexico for a decade, with little in the way of resources. His approach to the sport was as unconventional as his career path—Dorozhenko applied his grounding in math and science to come up with a hockey development program. He did his own research, and his decade in the Mexican national program was effectively his lab work with the rawest young athletes.

Dorozhenko later settled in Phoenix, and he started to work with Auston when the boy was seven. For a time, he even lived with Brian Matthews's parents. "Normally, I didn't work with players so young," Dorozhenko said. "I didn't know what to expect. Auston was so small. And with young kids, you wonder if you can keep their attention or if they'll get discouraged by the first time that they face adversity. You wonder if they're even going to come back a second time. That wasn't the case with Auston, not from day one. He listened. He asked questions because he wanted to understand exactly why we were doing drills, exercises—he was inquisitive about all aspects of the game."

Dorozhenko didn't spoon-feed or settle for baby steps with Auston. Workouts were four or five times a week during the summer, when, he said, Auston built his base. During the winter, the hockey season, they went onto the ice less often, working only on technical or mechanical adjustments so that Matthews could stay fresh for games.

By the time Auston was ten, his workload—each practice stretching up to two hours long—was demanding enough that it would have challenged older, much more seasoned athletes. Russ Courtnall, considered one of the NHL's best skaters during his fifteen-year career, later enrolled his son in Dorozhenko's program and, according to Dorozhenko, once tried and failed to get through a workout. Dorozhenko paid attention to the players' fatigue and muscle soreness, but none of it fazed Auston. His threshold for work was seemingly limitless. "He couldn't get enough," Dorozhenko said. "We worked out one-on-one, sometimes at six a.m. so that we could get ice. Auston would hop onto the ice with older players in their groups, competing all the time."

Dorozhenko believed that "trust is the foundation" of his relationship with Auston and his parents, and he didn't see himself simply as a coach of a young phenom, nor one player in the business of the game. "I consider Brian my brother. [The Matthewses] mean so much to me. They are family. Maybe it would feel different for me other places, but here, it's a small hockey community in a big urban area, so everyone knows everybody. People get along because everyone puts the interests of the kids first."

The seats at the Gila River Arena were filled mostly by fans in Coyotes sweaters, a large number of them kids, as the Leafs' only visit to the desert coincided with the Coyotes' Youth Hockey Night. A healthy portion, however, was freckled by blue Leafs sweaters, fairly exclusively Matthews's No. 34. It was a night Matthews had to share with one of his own heroes growing up, Shane Doan. It was Doan's 1,500th career NHL game, which moved him past Mike Modano into seventeenth place all-time. Before the season was out, he'd play forty more, pushing him ahead of Steve Yzerman and Brendan Shanahan. Doan's career was a measure of his loyalty to the franchise—effectively, the story of his career is the history of the Coyotes franchise itself. Only two players ahead of him on the list of all-time games played—Alex Delvecchio and Nicklas Lidstrom—had spent their entire careers with a single franchise.

Doan's landmark was recognized in a pregame ceremony. The honours then carried over into the opening action. Mike Babcock chose to put Matthews's line out for the opening face-off. Though he'd suppressed sentimental urges on almost every other occasion, this time the coach caved, his heart overruling anything that video or analytics might have told him.

"We want him to walk out of here proud," Babcock told the Postmedia Network. "I want him to soak it up and enjoy the whole thing."

Arizona coach Dave Tippett played along, sending out the line of Martin Hanzal, Tobias Rieder, and Shane Doan. He went even further, giving Doan, a right-winger, the honour of taking not just an honorary puck-drop but also the live, in-game opening draw against the kid who had skated with the Coyotes those summers not so long ago. At centre ice, the forty-year-old stood opposite the teenager who had worshipped him in grade school. Nothing could have better captured Doan's impact on the game in Arizona; nothing could have made Matthews's homecoming richer to him.

Though Matthews had come into the game on a roll, scoring six goals in nine games in the month of December, the fans were more desperate to see Doan find the back of the net. Another landmark was within reach: Doan was sitting on 399 career goals.

There was no magical beginning, not for Matthews, nor for Doan. The opening shift passed uneventfully. It didn't take long for Matthews to show his skills and shape the game. Just over three minutes into the game, Hanzal had a chance to move the puck out of the Coyotes zone, but Matthews surgically stripped him of the puck inside the Arizona blueline. Matthews quickly hit Connor Brown with a pass that he roofed in one touch, beating netminder Mike Smith to give the Leafs a 1–0 lead. Though the Coyotes carried the play to the Leafs through twenty minutes, the visitors carried the lead into the first intermission.

Toronto went on a power play early in the second period and, though he didn't earn an assist, Matthews set in motion the play that gave the Leafs a two-goal lead. On the halfboards, Matthews threaded a pass through traffic to Brown, who stood in the slot. Brown pushed the puck back to Jake Gardiner, and his slap shot from the point was deflected into the net by Leo Komarov, who stood at the edge of Smith's crease.

Doan finally had his moment in the last minute of the second period. Peter Holland—who had been traded from Toronto to Arizona earlier in the month—started the play in the Arizona end, and then Connor Murphy hit Doan with a pass that landed on his stick at the edge of Frederik Andersen's crease. Matthews had a great view of it—he had been caught up the ice, and his mentor had slipped behind him. After Doan buried the puck behind Andersen, the crowd erupted, evolving into a long, loud standing ovation, including Ema and Brian Matthews and the players on the Coyotes bench. That no one on the Leafs' bench acknowledged the milestone didn't escape the notice of Coyotes defenceman Oliver Ekman-Larsson, who chirped at the visitors as the teams lined up for the face-off at centre ice.

It wasn't quite a laugher in the third period. Andersen was tested a few times, but Doan's goal was the only one of 32 shots that would beat him. In the third, Komarov stretched the lead to 3–1 with an unassisted breakaway that he finished with a neat deke. And William Nylander added an insurance goal with a spectacular backhand on a breakaway to end his thirteen-game goalless drought.

The Coyotes had billed the game as a tribute to Doan and a celebration of youth hockey in the region—the past and the future of the game. Doan seemed to recognize the narrative of the night. Ever the humble professional, he was more than willing to share the spotlight with Matthews.

"What a great night for him; he's been amazing for our state," Doan said. "I've gotten to know him. I'm pretty proud of him."

The Leafs headed into their Christmas break with fourteen wins on the season, enough to keep them in the mix but still a far cry from a playoff spot. Doan and the Coyotes might have had one eye on the past that night, but for the Leafs, it was only the future that mattered.

CHAPTER SIX

AUSTON MATTHEWS HAD CAUGHT A BREAK WITH THE SCHED-ule. It wasn't just being on hand for Shane Doan's 400th goal in his 1,500th game. No, the way the schedule played out, he wouldn't even have to call a cab to make his way home for Christmas dinner. It was the first time in three years he was able to be home with his parents and his sister over the holidays, as he had spent the two previous Christmas seasons with the U.S. team at the world juniors.

After Christmas, the Leafs were back out on the road for another week, but Matthews could still get by in his preferred uniform of shorts and flip-flops. The team was convening in Fort Lauderdale, Florida, for a game against the Panthers and then going on to Tampa for a date with the Lightning. As midwinter road trips go, this was a prolonged one but made necessary by another hockey show that was landing in Toronto.

For the second time in three years, the Leafs were being displaced from the ACC due to the IIHF World Junior Championships. Matthews and Nylander had played in 2015's tournament, as had three Marlies: Kasperi Kapanen; lanky centre Frédérik Gauthier, the Leafs' first-round pick in 2013; and Rinat Valiev, a Russian defenceman selected a couple of rounds after Gauthier.

For those who follow the Leafs, the tournament wasn't quite the compelling interest it had been in the two previous years. The under-20s provide an opportunity to get an early read on an organization's two previous drafts. NHL scouting staffs that draft well tend to have at least four or five players on various rosters in the ten-team event. The Leafs had only one high-profile prospect: U.S. winger Jeremy Bracco, who had played the last two seasons with the Kitchener Rangers in the OHL. They also had one of the more entertaining players in the tournament, Martins Dzierkals of Latvia, a nervy rink rat the Leafs had drafted out of Riga two years ago.

A couple of asterisks had to be attached to Toronto's prospect pool at the event that featured games at the ACC before the medal round played out in Montreal. For one, the Leafs' best players who were eligible for the tournament, Matthews and Marner, were in the top three in NHL rookie scoring. Second, and slightly more compli-cated, the Leafs took an unusual approach to their draft after select-ing Matthews with the first overall pick, focusing on players who had passed through the draft in their first or second years of eligibility. Some of these older draftees (called by some Draft+1s and Draft+2s) were ineligible. For example, Yegor Korshkov, a Russian winger who had been selected with the first pick of the second round the previ-ous June, had a 1996 birthday, and the cutoff for the 2016 tourna-ment was January 1, 1997.

Perhaps the member of the Leafs organization who made the biggest splash at the world juniors was Mike Babcock, who coached the Canadian team at the 1997 tournament in Switzerland. For a few coaches—Babcock among them—a gold at the world juniors turns out to be a career-making break; for others, anything short of a gold leaves a smudge on their record that they can't erase. When Hockey Canada had tabbed Babcock for the job, he had been working well outside the spotlight: a couple of seasons with Moose Jaw in the Western Hockey League, a year with the University of Lethbridge, and then on to Spo-kane, also in the WHL. His Spokane team had attracted some atten-tion in junior-hockey circles when it put together a 104-point season with less than a star-studded line-up. It didn't help that Babcock was coming in at a time of maximum pressure: Canada had won five consecutive golds at the tournament, without even suffering a tie or loss over that stretch. He was also coming in with a roster of very average talent relative to those championship teams. Despite a few nervous moments—a two-goal third-period deficit in the semifinals against Russia—Babcock's squad squeezed all the juice out of the lemon and, in turn, the coach won immediate industry respect.

With a world junior, a Stanley Cup, and two Olympic golds, Babcock owns a CV that matches that of anyone in the game, although his salary with the Leafs outstrips them all. Of all the tournament alumni in the Leafs' room, only Babcock and Zaitsev own golds from the world juniors. If Canada had crashed and burned—like it had when Marner played for the team—Mike Babcock might have had to wait a long time for his shot at the pros, if it ever came at all.

After some desultory results by American teams in the International Ice Hockey Federation's under-20 tournaments, USA Hockey took a bold initiative in 1996 and launched its national development program in Ann Arbor, Michigan, for players under the age of eighteen. The strategy behind USA Hockey's NTDP (National Team Development Program) was plain: Recruit the top teenage talent in the country, bring them together with better resources and competition than they'd get at home, and expose them to the best available coaching. In its first years, the USNTDP had mixed results, but then the program started to win international gold, first at the under-18s in 2002, and then, with largely the same group of players, at the under-20s in 2004. U.S. teams were a major factor in IIHF tournaments consistently in the years following, and while Matthews was skating with the Bobcats, he tracked the team.

"There were the Coyotes, his favourites, but Ann Arbor was like his other home team," Ema Matthews says. "It was always his goal to get there, and really a family goal. We used all of our vacations taking him to tournaments in L.A. or Las Vegas or in the Northeast. It was so that he could play in Ann Arbor someday and play for the American teams."

USA Hockey scouted age-group tournaments, so Auston Matthews was on its radar going back at least to his bantam year, maybe even earlier. Don Granato was coaching the USNTDP's under-18 team when USA Hockey extended an invitation to Matthews, then age fifteen, and his father for a visit ahead of tryouts for the next fall's under-17 team. Granato had never seen Matthews play, live or on video, but he had heard reports from the USNTDP staff that had been tracking him. He had thought Arizona was an unlikely place to produce a prospect for the program. He also knew that the Everett Silvertips had drafted Matthews in the third round of the WHL's 2012 bantam draft.

Granato was completing his work with the '95s and would be taking over the '97s the next season. He liked to give visiting kids from the incoming class a chance to skate with an older group, in this case a group of players who were just weeks away from the NHL entry draft. Sometimes prospects that Granato put in that position struggled to keep up, and others were overcome by audition anxiety. Matthews, however, made a first and lasting impression on Granato. You couldn't pick out the underage player from the older ones around him.

"It wasn't just that he could keep up or even excel," Granato said. "It was his attitude and body language. All of it said, 'I belong here. I can do this. I can play. I can excel.' It's a huge step up. . . . A lot of very good players try to make that step in the workouts—I remember Dylan Larkin and Jack Eichel doing it. But none had made the transition as quickly as Auston. It seemed like he was there right from the drop of the puck."

After the practice, Granato went straight to the program's scouts and said, "Tell me that you have this kid signed for next year." Some of the most heavily recruited kids, those who had options to go to major junior teams in Canada or teams in the United States Hockey League, were given full commitments before the tryouts. Granato was concerned that the prospect might wind up going to the state of Washington to play major junior with Everett. When the scouts told Granato that Matthews was coming to tryouts for the under-17 team in a few weeks, the coach reiterated the point, with a heightened sense of urgency: "No, I'm not asking about the tryouts or anything. Just tell me that you have that kid signed up for the fall."

Matthews made the cut and more in the tryouts, and Granato knew he had a team that was absolutely loaded with talent compared to other birth years in the program. Matthews wasn't the big story when USA Hockey announced its roster for the under-17 team. Write-ups in newspapers and online focused on Caleb Jones, the younger brother of Seth Jones, who had been the fourth overall pick in the 2013 NHL draft. The pair were the sons of Popeye Jones, the former NBA veteran, and they had first picked up the game of hockey when their father was playing in Denver. That Matthews wasn't bigger news was in part a function of his coming from off the traditional grid. If he had played in Detroit, as Patrick Kane had as a teenager, he would have come in with a profile; if he had been from Boston, like Jack Eichel, he would have been better known. But although Matthews flew under the media radar, he quickly established himself with the coaching staff.

"For me," said Granato, "within three or four days, it was 'Oh my gosh.' We have a lot of special players. This Matthews kid is a spectacular player."

Matthews and his parents had worked towards this moment, but still, sending him to Michigan tested them. "It was tough to see him go, to move away," Ema said. "For Auston, I'm sure it was tough, too. I'm sure he was more homesick when he left than he let us know. I know he hated the weather. But it was a chance to practice and play every day. He really had gone as far as he could here in Arizona. He always had a sense of purpose, and this was what he was going to have to do."

Matthews had not yet turned sixteen when he and Luke Opilka, a goaltender with the under-17s, moved into the home of Brian and Heidi Daniels and their two sons in a suburb of Ann Arbor. "Our two sons are younger than Auston, and because he grew up with sisters, I think he liked the idea of being the older brother to our boys," Heidi Daniels said. "It changed the dynamic for sure—our older boy would pick on the younger, but with Auston there, it was like there was a new sheriff in town."

The Daniels family had never hosted players from the USNTDP before, and they didn't know exactly what they had signed on for. For the most part, the players were, Heidi said, "respectful and well behaved." They strayed from Boy Scout mode on occasion—Heidi and Brian still talk about the time they left their sons at home with Matthews and Opilka and returned early to find them leaning out of a second-floor window, trying to sink shots into the basketball hoop in the driveway. Nonetheless, they were model guests and let off surplus steam in the basement playing hockey with the younger Daniels boys—not mini-sticks but full-on games.

Matthews had barely settled into the Ann Arbor program and the Daniels home when it seemed like his season was imperiled. Just a couple of weeks in, in just their second game, the under-17s took on an all-star team from the NAJHL, and Matthews went to the net on what seemed like an innocent play. He took a knee-on-knee hit on the open ice. Granato said that at first he didn't think it was serious. "I've seen guys walk away from a lot worse," the coach said. But Opilka, who was in net for the team at the far end of the ice, knew that it spelled trouble. "It was a dirty hit. What I remember was the sound it made. That was the scariest part. I knew it was serious."

Matthews broke his left femur. Surgeons inserted a pin in his leg and fitted him for a cast. He came back to his billets' home on crutches, and when he finally made it to school the next week, his teammates pushed him to classes in a wheelchair. The fracture specialists told Matthews and the USA Hockey coaches that he was going to be on the sidelines for three months, and that was if his recovery went as planned.

"It was a hard day when the team called and we got the news," Ema Matthews says. "It was the first time he had a serious injury. We hadn't been through anything like it."

"There was a thought that maybe Auston would go back to Arizona while he recovered, but he stayed with us," Heidi Daniels says. "I know it was hard for him when the team went on road trips and he had to stay at home, but I think that might have helped him settle in with us."

In his months on the sidelines, Matthews's No. 34 sweater—the lowest number on the roster among skaters—hung in his stall. He could have fallen behind his teammates in conditioning and acclimating to an environment more competitive than they had ever skated in before. He could have grown disappointed, dispirited, and even anxious. That was always in the back of the minds of the team's coaching staff. But Matthews went entirely in the opposite direction. "I've seen it with other players before—not many, but it happens," Granato said. "Auston got better when he was out of the line-up."

Matthews came to the rink every day and made the extra effort to stay part of the team. It was more than just hanging around and killing time, however. Some of it was symbolic but still meaningful to his teammates—sometimes his cast didn't permit him to travel on the team bus to road games, but when the team returned to the home arena, Matthews was waiting in the parking lot. Some of it amounted to taking on homework—he sat in on every players' meeting, picked the brains of the coaches who screened videos for the team and individual players, and watched video on his own time. "Auston didn't have a chance to get onto the ice and go through it, not with a pin sticking out of his leg, but he did get a better understanding of what the coaches were asking the players to do, as much as anyone in the line-up and on the ice," said his coach. "Auston soaked up the information like a sponge."

Matthews's recovery went as scheduled, but he was still out of the line-up for three full months. At first he was cleared for light skating and worked on the ice with the goalie coach. When he returned to full practice in December, he was in what should have been a disadvantaged position. As months pass, the pace of play picks up for players of all ages—it's a simple matter of their conditioning raised to its highest level through daily practice and games. Matthews was reentering completely cold when his teammates were revving and hitting on all cylinders with a rolling start. He should have had to play catch-up. It turned out to be exactly the opposite.

"Auston's first game back was against Dubuque, one of the stronger teams in the USHL that season," recalled Granato. "The weekend before [Auston came back] our kids had a 2–1 lead against Dubuque with ten minutes to go and wound up losing 5–2. It was a real tough loss for them on the road. Dubuque had an older, bigger team. They took it to us. The way the schedule was set up was a little odd. We were back in Dubuque the very next weekend, this time with Auston. And our kids were in exactly the same situation they had been in the previous weekend: defending a 2–1 lead against an older team in a hostile environment. It looked like it was going to be history repeating itself—Dubuque scored two goals in two minutes and took a 3–2 lead. I called a timeout and pulled all our guys in to the bench and then I didn't say anything. [Team captain] Luke Kunin did all the talking. Auston didn't say anything, but he took it all in. It was like he had been waiting all that time just for this moment. The puck is dropped, and seven seconds later, Auston makes a play to set up Christian Fischer for a goal. Seven seconds! It's 3–3, and there's another face-off. Twenty seconds later it's Auston scoring. We went on to hold the lead and win the game, and afterwards I'm thinking: *Did that really happen? This is really his first time through this with the team, probably the first time he played a game in front of a crowd.* I just said to one of my assistants: 'That's a statement that kid made.'"

Matthews's first game back was a portent of what was to come. Just weeks after the win in Dubuque, the U.S. '97s played in its showcase tournament, the World Under-17 Challenge, a Hockey Canada event that brings in top international age-group teams and squads selected from top Canadian leagues. Sydney, Nova Scotia, hosted the tournament, and the Americans rolled through the competition undefeated, capping their run with a 9–1 pounding of Quebec in the semifinals and a one-sided 4–0 win over Team Pacific in the gold-medal game.

Matthews centred a line between Matthew Tkachuk, son of NHL veteran Keith Tkachuk, and Jack Roslovic. Matthews didn't lead the team in scoring—that honour went to Colin White—but he did make an impression on a veteran NHL scout who had seen more than a dozen under-17 tournaments. "He was your prototype of an NHL franchise centreman," the scout said. "There was a little more projection involved with him being a late birthday, nine months younger than a lot of the kids, but he was in control when he was out there."

Over the course of USHL games and exhibitions after the

Under-17 Challenge, Matthews separated himself even from the elite forwards on the roster. He practiced with the under-18 team and made his debut as an underager in a game against Michigan State University, whose roster featured twenty-two- and twenty-three-year-old upperclassmen, experienced collegians. Despite being five or six years younger than the Spartans, Matthews picked up a goal in a 4–3 win for the U.S. team. He passed his audition and would stick with the U-18s through to the worlds in April. In twenty games playing up in Ann Arbor, Matthews scored twelve times, including goals in wins over Sweden in the world semifinals and the Czechs in the gold-medal game.

At the season's end, Granato's assessment was plain: With Matthews returning the next fall to rejoin the rest of the 1997 class, the coach was going to work with one of the three best teams that USA Hockey had ever put on the ice. "It was a strong group of players, and they all pushed themselves to be better every day. One player's competitiveness made another kid that much more competitive, right down the line. Auston was at the centre of that. He was out to make himself better every day, no matter what, and from that first time he skated with the '95s he never let down, not once."

When Matthews, an inch taller and fifteen pounds heavier, returned to Scottsdale after his first season in Ann Arbor, Boris Dorozhenko could see a physically different teenager than the one who had left to play in the USNTDP. He could hear the change from boy to man. "He said to me, 'Hey, Boris,'" Dorozhenko said, affecting a basso profundo. "Working with him is going to be different, I figured. Now he is like a professional, and there are no limits."

In the summer of 2014, Matthews again skated with Shane Doan and the Coyotes at the team's practice facility. He was the kid from the

Bobcats no longer; not a kid at all, in fact. "His reputation preceded him," Doan said. "It didn't change anything the way he worked out with us, though. There was nothing that suggested he was caught up in his success with the U.S. program. He was just Auston, the kid who skated with us, bigger and better than ever. He had the game and the attitude for the next level. He seemed pretty aware of where he was going."

It seemed that way when the *Arizona Republic* sent out a reporter to talk to him at the Ice Den. He told the reporter that he had bigger ambitions than just making it to the NHL. "Someday I want to be that role model for kids from Arizona that you can play hockey and do well at it," Matthews said.

Don Granato was around Matthews on a day-to-day basis going into his second season, but the coach read Matthews slightly differently than Doan: If Matthews never came off like a kid or a starstruck hockey fan around the Coyotes, it was only because he could hide it well. In his second year with Matthews, Granato knew that he had to prepare the burgeoning star for the professional life on and off the ice. The teenager wasn't young for his age—he just wasn't any more mature than you'd expect any kid turning eighteen to be. Granato thought it was important for his elite players to get a sense of what the NHL life was like, so he would take Matthews and others to Red Wings games at Joe Louis Arena, capitalizing on a family connection—his brother Tony Granato, who worked as an assistant coach to Detroit coach Mike Babcock.

After a game against Philadelphia, Don Granato took Matthews downstairs to meet Babcock, and they waited in the players' family room until summoned for the audience with the coach. When they finally got the call, they walked through the halls under the stands, and Matthews spotted Flyers star Claude Giroux in his street clothes on his cell phone.

"Can I get a picture with him?" Matthews asked.

Granato gave him a flat and emphatic no. "Don't you dare," he said.

Matthews was startled by it, but Granato explained it in painful detail. "You're going to play in the league someday," he said. "You have to wait until Claude Giroux asks to get a picture with you." Granato wanted to get Matthews over it—he knew Matthews was going to have to play against Giroux and other famous names in the league, and that it would be all business out there. "You have to be better than Claude Giroux or whoever it is that you're on the ice against," Granato said. "There are no fans out there." There was still a kid inside Auston for sure, but he soon got past that.

Though Matthews and his linemates Matthew Tkachuk and Jack Roslovic were back for a second season, the 2014–15 under-18s lost a couple of significant talents when defencemen Noah Hanifin and Zach Werenski accelerated their high school studies and moved straight to college. Still, the core of the powerhouse under-17s returned and picked up where they had left off. Early in the fall, Matthews scored twice in the US-18s' 6–4 exhibition loss at Boston University. It was a quality loss—BU featured Jack Eichel, the star of the U.S. under-18 team the previous season, the second-ranked prospect eligible for the 2015 NHL entry draft behind only Connor McDavid, and the eventual winner of the Hobey Baker Award as the top player in U.S. college hockey. Moreover, BU was more than the Jack Eichel Show, as the team made it all the way to the NCAA final.

Matthews built on his showing against BU. Weeks later, he scored twice, including the overtime winner, against No. 4–ranked Minnesota in Minneapolis. He racked up another pair of goals in a 4–1 win at the University of Wisconsin.

"When you got down to it," said one NHL senior amateur scout, "Matthews wasn't playing so often against college players, as Eichel was. But he was about as effective with a much younger supporting cast. There wasn't much to pick between them at that point, and when you considered that Matthews was a full year younger, you'd have to say he was probably even more impressive."

The main midwinter attraction again featured Matthews playing up: the 2015 IIHF under-20s in Montreal and Toronto. Again, just like in his first workout at Ann Arbor, Matthews was skating with players older and more experienced than he was. Still, the buzz around the tournament focused on McDavid and Eichel—McDavid was the prohibitive favourite to be the first overall pick in the 2015 draft, but a lot of hockey fans, not just those cheering for the U.S. team, were hoping to see tears in Superboy's cape. It was a ten-team tournament, but you'd never know it from looking at the sports pages or listening to chatter in online chat rooms. Matthews managed to come in somewhat under the radar, even though he was having a bigger, better season in Ann Arbor than he had with the under-17s. The general manager of the American squad, Jim Johannson, didn't hesitate to talk up Matthews's stock, calling him "a special player," but it seemed as though no one even heard him. On more than one occasion, after practice or after games, Eichel would be standing in front of dozens of reporters, taking questions, while Matthews stood just a few feet away, getting next to no attention. While the USA Hockey program might seem egalitarian—giving Matthews a chance to play as an underager on the U-18 team the previous season and giving Eichel exactly the same opportunity the year before that—there's still an entrenched hierarchy in the organization. Those who sign on and put in their time will get their turn when the time comes. This was Eichel's turn. This was the turn for the '95 birthdays. Matthews was to play a supporting role—he was assigned the role of third-line centre and was going to have to wait to get his star turn, to be the featured player in coming tournaments.

Matthews got off to a rough start. In an early game against Finland, a shot deflected off him into his own net. When the United States met Canada in the opening round, the hosts beat their chief rivals, and the media scored the game a win for McDavid over Eichel, paying little notice to Matthews. The Americans hoped to get a second bite at the Canadians in the gold-medal game but crashed out in the quarterfinals. Although the Americans roundly outplayed Russia, the U.S. juniors ran into a hot goaltender. Despite the team's quick exit, Matthews made an impression on NHL scouts: Many thought that, even in his lesser role, Matthews had had a better tournament than Eichel.

Matthews's stock continued to climb throughout his under-18 season, reaching its peak that spring at the under-18 tournament in Lucerne and Zug in Switzerland. Matthews exacted a bit of revenge for the loss to Canada at the world juniors by scoring the go-ahead and winning goals in a 7–2 rout of Canada in the semis. The final was a tight game against the Finns, and midway through the third period the United States trailed 1–0. Matthews set up his linemate Jack Roslovic for the tying goal, and the Americans won the game in overtime on a goal by Colin White, thus going undefeated in international play across their two years in the USNTDP and giving the program its sixth title in seven years.

Matthews led all scorers in Switzerland, with 8 goals and 7 assists in seven games. He swept the awards: tournament MVP, best forward, and a spot on the all-star team. He ranked fourth on the USNTDP's list of leaders in career scoring—his 167 points trailed only Phil Kessel (180), Patrick Kane (172), and Matthews's teammate Jeremy Bracco (168). If he hadn't missed three months with injury, he would have shattered Kessel's record. Although Eichel's run at Boston University and his Hobey Baker Award stole a lot of Matthews's thunder for U.S. hockey fans, those in the USNTDP staff considered his run in the program the most impressive in Ann Arbor's history. He had thrived in his two years there, and as Dorozhenko noted, he had developed "mature strength" with the hours he had put in at the gym, and mental strength also.

And yet, after all that, Matthews still felt at a bit of a dead end, as though his options were limited. He felt he was ready for the NHL, but the NHL was not ready for him. No USNTDP player had ever gone directly from Ann Arbor to the NHL. Those who would have been likely candidates—Kane, Kessel, and Eichel—were, like Matthews, born after September 15 and thus not eligible for the NHL draft, while the rest of the kids born earlier in their birth years heard their names called. Born on September 17, Matthews missed out on the big dance by only two days. He was going to have to bide his time, though he really didn't want to have to settle for that.

Elite players coming out of the USNTDP have two clear and distinct paths in their draft year. One: They can go to the Canadian Hockey League and play a season of major junior, as Patrick Kane did when he put in a year with the London Knights. The CHL is the most tried-and-true career path for those who would be stars—when the NHL announced its First and Second All-Star Teams at the end of the 2013–14 season, eight of the twelve players came out of the CHL. For many American kids, Kane being a prime example, there was a familiarity to the CHL game.

Two: Elite teens can land a scholarship with an NCAA program. Matthews could have followed Eichel's lead, and historically, USNTDP execs liked to see their players go the college route. USA Hockey champions the NCAA game, and its staff maintains tight relationships with the coaches in the established schools. For most kids in the USNTDP, the college game is what they know. Growing up in Boston, Eichel had attended dozens of college games, and likewise Kessel in Wisconsin. They didn't land at their favourite schools—a

Boston College fan, Eichel spent a season at Boston University, and Kessel stirred some local controversy when he jilted the hometown school and played for the University of Minnesota. College seemed to be the likeliest option for Matthews, so when the under-18 team made its rounds of schools for exhibitions that season, rumours circulated: Matthews's short list was supposed to include the University of North Dakota, Boston College, Boston University, Michigan, and Denver.

Matthews wasn't in a position to pick and choose, however. The Everett Silvertips had taken him in the third round of the 2012 bantam draft. "He's one of those big-time pieces we're hoping might fall our way," Silvertips general manager Garry Davidson told the Everett *Herald* after drafting Matthews.

Practicing year-round, logging thousands of hours in hockey school, playing in international tournaments in his mid-teens—Matthews's story was a piece of the game as we had come to know it. He was born before the new millennium, but he was the model of a twenty-first-century player—he was the future. It seemed fitting, then, that the Toronto Maple Leafs' biggest midseason event on the schedule was a throwback to a distant past. It had taken Matthews only sixty minutes to make NHL history. Now he was about to step into it.

CHAPTER SEVEN

THE NHL'S CENTENNIAL CLASSIC WAS AN AWKWARD EVENT TO stage-manage. Scheduling it for January 1, 2017, felt like a fudge. The puck was dropped at the NHL's first game not a century before—technically, it was ninety-nine years and two months ago. That first game in the newly minted league was played between Toronto and Montreal—then the Wanderers, not even the Canadiens. But the Canadiens had already celebrated their hundredth-anniversary season over two whole seasons and hosted their own centennial game back in 2009 when they played Boston. The Canadiens' hundredth birthday was the biggest party in the modern history of the league, and the Leafs hadn't been invited. Was it a snub, or was the same thinking involved for January 1, 2017?

So it was that the Leafs' opponent at the Winter Classic would be Detroit, not Montreal. The league likes to keep its background politics opaque. Maybe Montreal's presence would have made it feel like the Canadiens' centenary all over again. Certainly the involvement of the national rival risked stealing the thunder of the home team. Awarding the league's signature midseason event to Toronto represented a leap of faith, a vote of confidence, or a bit of both. The optics couldn't be worse if the host of the classic were at the bottom of the league or in full-on tank mode once more. No doubt there was palpable relief in the NHL offices when Matthews scored four goals in Ottawa in the season opener. *At least they'll be interesting come January.*

Detroit was going through a rebuild of its own and didn't have any established star power—Dylan Larkin was in a somewhat analogous position to Matthews, but there was no billing the game as a head-to-head showdown, not like the league brass had when they rolled out Ovechkin versus Crosby when the Penguins hosted the game in 2011.

The decision was wisely made to keep the scale of the venue appropriate. You might not consider BMO Field intimate, but with its twenty-seven-thousand-seat capacity, it was intimate indeed by comparison to some past venues for the NHL's marquee game. The first Winter Classic was played in Buffalo's Rich Stadium, which seats eighty thousand. The closest thing to that in Toronto would have been the Rogers Centre, with its fifty-thousand-seat capacity for baseball, and the Leafs could have easily sold it out if a pure cash-grab were all that they had had in mind. But aesthetics were a key factor. The Rogers Centre has an enclosed feeling; even with the roof open, it has the feeling of a domed stadium. BMO would give the Centennial Classic more of an open-air, winter ambience. The view of the city skyline and the waterfront made it feel more in and of Toronto. A soccer venue also put the spectators that much closer to the rink constructed on the field. And the same rang true for the television cameras.

To mark its centennial, the league put together an expert panel to draw up a list of the one hundred greatest players in NHL history. It was a perfect conversation point. How do you strike a balance between the stars of the modern game with those from the 1920s and '30s, who are known only as names in old clippings and the record books? Who among the modern game's stars are most deserving? In the pregame of the Centennial Classic, the league unveiled the first thirty-three players from its list, the stars of the NHL's first fifty years. *Hockey Night in Canada*'s Ron MacLean introduced the first twenty-eight, each of whom was represented by his children and grandchildren. Some fought back tears, and all received warm applause. The last five, all now in their eighties and nineties, came out and acknowledged the crowd. The league's choice to save the modern-era picks for the NHL All-Star Game in Los Angeles in a few weeks' time was judicious, and it reminded everyone at BMO Field that no one on the ice that afternoon was in the conversation to be among the league's top one hundred. Henrik Zetterberg had the most impressive CV of anybody in the Centennial Classic—he won the Conn Smythe Trophy when the Wings last won the Stanley Cup, but he had never been voted to a First or Second All-Star Team in his fourteen-year career. By comparison, the old-timers game between Detroit and Toronto alumni the day before had been absolutely star-studded: four former Red Wings in that game would make the list of the NHL's one hundred greatest (Shanahan, Chelios, Coffey, and Lidstrom), along with two Leafs (Sittler and Salming). Five other players in the old-timers game fell short of the top one hundred but have their plaques in the Hockey Hall of Fame as consolation (Murphy and Larionov for Detroit; Gilmour, Sundin, and McDonald for Toronto).

The pregame ceremonies ran longer than any single period of the game would in real time. Longer than any period and intermission, in fact. The broadcasters at *Hockey Night in Canada* and the NHL Network gave sponsors their money's worth. The broadcasters were also counting on the fans' embracing history and their insatiable appetite for sentimentality and lore. Besides, those who were paying upwards of four figures for the choicest seats would expect something more than sixty minutes of hockey and thirty-six minutes of loops from the Zambonis.

By the time the ceremonies had wrapped up, it was already dinnertime. The sun was setting, and only a thin strip of the west-facing stands had to squint to look out at the ice surface. The rest of the fans in the shade pulled their jackets tighter as the temperatures dipped.

To its credit, though, the crowd never let any impatience be known. Still, when the teams finally assembled on the ice for the puck-drop, there was a palpable sense of relief. Some of the trappings were a little out of the ordinary. The coaches were wearing team jackets like you might see on bantam coaches and boosters at a local rink. If the players were going with an extra layer, it wasn't plain to the eye. This wasn't extreme cold like when the Canadiens and the Oilers faced off and goalie Jose Theodore played with a thermal ski cap.

The puck-drop was the last ceremony, a split-second one: Zetterberg and Matthews out for the opening face-off, the night's most distinguished veteran against its brightest emerging star. If it was a scripted passing of the torch, it was only written when the coaches filled out their line-ups and named their starters.

Once the puck was dropped, however, those in the stands and the rest watching the game at home or online were treated to hockey of a mostly conventional sort. A couple of shifts into the contest, as Nazem Kadri carried the puck in the Wings end, defenceman Brendan Smith struggled to keep up and tripped him to head off a scoring chance, earning himself a trip to the box. Though the Leafs came in having scored five power-play goals in the four previous games, they didn't generate a solid scoring chance through the two minutes. Early in the man advantage, Marner walked off the wall and fired a shot, but it couldn't get through traffic to the Detroit net. Matthews then came out on the second power-play unit, but the second team didn't have much of an impact.

Though the league had trumpeted the idea that the ice quality for the Centennial Classic was going to be the best ever for an outdoor game, it still seemed like it was a little off compared to the surface in controlled conditions. Cross-ice passes wobbled, and the puck fluttered when stickhandled. The ice seemed to give a bit when the players tried to explode from a stop or make a sharp turn in stride.

Players are creatures of routine, and even the slightest thing can disrupt them—and a game played outdoors is no slight thing. The lighting was much different than a standard NHL arena's, and the vast open spaces outside the boards were unsettling, even disorienting. No surprise, then, that the first twenty minutes were fairly mundane: a period not of feeling out the other team so much as acclimatizing to the new conditions. It wasn't end-to-end action, more station-to-station. Neither team dominated possession or sustained pressure. Still, it had to rate as a good start for the Leafs. More of the Wings players had been through an NHL outdoor experience, and their key players had a wealth of big-game experience earned through deep runs in the playoffs. Moreover, the visitors seemed to have more motivation, more on the line—the game represented a vital two points after a dismal start to their season. The Wings might have had an aging core, but in the preseason, the team had been presumed to make the playoffs, just as every Detroit team had going back to the 1990–91 season. Many questioned whether the setting, ceremony, and break from the routine would unsettle the young Leafs players. Through the first twenty minutes, they gave as good as they got, from Matthews and the two rookies on his flank—Hyman and Brown—right down to the fourth line, where Soshnikov and Gauthier skated with the designated tough guy, Matt Martin. For the lot of them, it seemed to be business as usual.

That lasted until the five-minute mark of the second period, when Zetterberg muscled Matthews off the puck at the Toronto blueline and then fed Anthony Mantha near the top of the circle on the right wing. Matthews skated out to get between Mantha and the net and went down not quite to his knees to block the shot, but the Detroit forward shifted a step back to have a clean sight line and buy time to load up on a snap shot. The puck found the top corner on Andersen's glove side. The goalie had been the Leafs' best player in the month of December, when the team made its run from the bottom of the conference standings. Mantha's shot was heavy and true, but Andersen had saved tougher in that stretch. After Detroit seized the lead, the crowd wasn't quite taken out of the game, but a hush fell, allowing the Wings' whooping to echo around the stadium. The Leafs' energy dipped noticeably after the goal. Toronto fans had long complained about the NHL awarding the outdoor game to other franchises. They'd finally gotten what they asked for, but now they couldn't help but feel a sense of dread that the big day would be another loss.

In the third period, however, the Leafs came out flying. Jake Gardiner, ever the wandering blueliner, wandered deep into the Wings' corner and threw a centring pass to Leo Komarov, who fought through the check of Nick Jensen and then pushed the puck past Jared Coreau. Just like that, the stadium was reenergized as the crowd celebrated the most meaningful goal scored outdoors in Toronto since those winters before the St. Pats' arena opened on Mutual Street in 1912.

Though the temperatures continued to drop as night fell, the game grew hot-blooded. A couple of borderline hits sparked a fight between Matt Martin and Steve Ott. The set-to resulted in about a dozen punches thrown, a minute-long wrestling session, and trash talking in the penalty boxes that lasted the duration of the five-minute majors.

As time wound down in the third period, it was clear that Babcock's confidence in Matthews's two-way game was growing—the coach was sending the rookie out for defensive-zone face-offs instead of Bozak, one of the league's best on the draw, or Kadri, the designated shut-down centre. You wouldn't have called it a high point in Matthews's game—NHL face-offs are won through veteran guile, elite hand-eye coordination, and bull strength—but Matthews was ahead of other teenage centres entering the league. Crosby and McDavid had both been regularly pushed off the puck in their rookie years. Matthews was holding his own against Zetterberg in the circle.

The Leafs took the lead with less than twelve minutes to go in the third period. Marner, carrying the puck, staying a stick length from checkers chasing him and surveying the ice for a linemate to skate into open ice, did almost a complete lap of the Detroit zone. The Red Wings out on the ice were at the end of a long shift, nearing a minute, when Marner walked out from the wall, pulled away from a weary Mantha, and fired the puck past Coreau.

So began a furious rally.

A minute later, Hyman scooped up a rebound and skated behind the Detroit net, grinding away and buying time until he spotted Brown in the slot. Brown's one-timer gave Toronto a two-goal lead.

Then, just a couple of shifts later, Brown found Matthews on the far right side during a three-on-one. Brown's pass was right on the tape, and Matthews wired a wrister past Coreau for his nineteenth goal of the season. Matthews's thirteen-game scoring drought suddenly seemed a long time ago; he was back on 40-goal pace.

The previous season, the Leafs hadn't won a single game when they had trailed going into the third period. This year, they had already managed it once in their first thirty-five games, and it looked like this one was safely in the bank, with the Leafs up 4–1. The thousands at BMO Field celebrated. Many in the expensive seats, as was their wont at the ACC, started making for the exits.

But the victory turned out to be far from a sure thing. Generations of fans will say that they were there for the historic end of this game, but be assured that many of them saw it only as an alert on their phones or heard the play-by-play on their car radios.

With less than six minutes to go, Detroit drew to within two on a goal by Johan Eriksson. Then, with the goaltender pulled for a sixth attacker and less than two minutes left, Tomas Tatar stole the puck in the Leafs' end. He fed it over to Zetterberg, who fired it on net. Andersen made the save, but Larkin, tearing towards the net, cashed in the rebound.

By now the Leafs fans were starting to recognize their recurring nightmare. The team was up by a goal with just over a minute to play. All they had to do was kill the clock. Easier said than done.

The sequence started with six Detroit skaters, sixty-three seconds to go, and a face-off between Matthews and Zetterberg outside the Leafs' blueline. Zetterberg won the draw, and the Wings kept possession the rest of the way. The Leafs couldn't get fresh legs on the ice—Matthews looked to be skating in quicksand. In the middle of the chaos, Morgan Rielly had a chance to clear the puck, but his stick broke and the Wings regained possession. Brown and Hyman both had their own opportunities to clear the zone, but the puck rolled on them, and the Wings kept them hemmed in. With less than two seconds left, in a goalmouth scramble, Mantha put the puck past Andersen. Confusion reigned—the game clock didn't stop, and the horn sounded. Babcock was trying to get the officials' attention, making a claim that the Wings had interfered with Andersen, but there was no hope. Detroit had tied the game.

Fifty years and counting of Leafs frustrations didn't make for a promising outlook to overtime, nor did Leafs experiences in extra time that season. In games that had gone to three-on-three that year, the Red Wings were 5-0 and the Leafs 1-5, their only win being their victory over McDavid and the Oilers.

Babcock sent Matthews, Brown, and Rielly out to open the five-minute overtime, and the teams exchanged long possessions with slow buildups to chances. Kadri had one chance early on. Then Marner took a pass from Rielly and missed the mark. With less than two minutes left, Rielly wound up with a clean breakaway but was turned aside by Coreau. The Wings had their chances, too. At one point Brown skated with all-out desperation the length of the ice to successfully break up a two-on-one.

It seemed that a shoot-out was an inevitability. And then Matthews stepped out onto the ice once more.

First, he carried the puck over the Detroit blueline, buttonhooked on the left wing, and dropped the puck for Gardiner. Matthews then skated hard to the net while Gardiner fired away, a shot that went four feet wide. The puck took a crazy carom off the end boards as Matthews cut across the front of the net. Danny DeKeyser tried to hold up Matthews, but as the puck bobbled out, Matthews fought off the check and, with one leg up in the air, backhanded the puck off Coreau's arm and into the net.

The horn from the ACC blasted at more than 100 decibels. On any other night, it would have reverberated off the arena's roof and been faintly audible only to those standing on the sidewalk or within earshot of Maple Leaf Square. But on that first night of the calendar year, the horn echoed out into the black ether above Lake Ontario. As one, the fans in their Maple Leafs sweaters leapt to their feet and erupted into cheers. The players poured over the boards and mobbed Matthews, while Babcock and his assistant coaches made their way off the ice. But the joyous moment was interrupted. The end couldn't have been better scripted, but the play had been challenged, and off-ice officials were reviewing the play to make sure that the Leafs hadn't entered the Detroit zone offside or interfered with the netminder. In the stands, behind the benches, on the ice, everyone held their places. Ten seconds passed, maybe a few more—fans didn't notice, as they were too busy watching the replay of Matthews's goal on the hi-def jumbotron. The players seemed to know what was coming, as they moved directly to the handshake line, and eventually it was made official: Matthews had won the day.

"It was a blast out there under the sun, the setting, a couple of Original Six teams going at it against each other. It was a pretty fun night," Matthews told nhl.com. "Definitely one of the best moments in hockey I've ever experienced. It's pretty special."

At nineteen, can anyone appreciate the history that came before themselves? For Auston Matthews, it wasn't just a matter of age. He had always been a student of the game—the physics, the science, maybe at some level the art. But what could he truly know of history? The NHL had no historical footprint in the desert sand. He had seen history unfold, but it was modern history. When Matthews first saw Wayne Gretzky, the Great One was the Coyotes' coach. Matthews almost certainly knew nothing about most of the names of the greats of yore who were honoured before the game. And the same goes for the other young Leafs. Eddie Shore is a name they heard dropped in *Slap Shot*, but what it meant, they'd have no way of knowing. What could they know of Howie Morenz? Did they get any sense of a city's enduring love of those from the 1967 team, Red Kelly and Johnny Bower? The Centennial Classic had lived up to the ceremony beforehand. The irony was that those who had starred in the action that afternoon might only fully realize the import of the event when they were old and gray.

CHAPTER EIGHT

THE WIN AT THE CENTENNIAL CLASSIC RAISED EXPECTATIONS to heights unforeseen back in October. The team that had been in the cellar a couple of weeks into the season was, if not in the penthouse with a rooftop pool, then at least in an upper-floor suite with a view of the playoffs. In a seven-game stretch over Christmas and into the new year, with the Centennial Classic the only home game, the Leafs had gone 6-0-1. The only point they had dropped was an overtime loss to the conference-leading Capitals in Washington. If the Leafs weren't the talk of hockey, at least people were talking about them, and, for once, not as objects of ridicule. It was serendipitous timing, too—it was only a week into the new year, but invitations to the All-Star Game in Los Angeles were already in the offing.

The voting caused a small tempest around the Leafs, one that again revolved around management attempting to create a team culture. The obvious candidate for selection to the All-Star Game was Auston Matthews, the team's leading scorer. Matthews was exactly the type of young star that the league wanted to showcase at the event—not to fans so much as corporate interests around the league. In recent years, the All-Star Game had become something of a league trade show, an opportunity for the players on the ice to meet the big players in business. Matthews's going to L.A. was billed as a treat for the fans, but really it was a benefit for the league.

This, however, ran counter to the approach that the Leafs had taken with all of their young players. The front office didn't want the kids' heads turned by media attention, something they viewed as a real risk given the saturated coverage of the team in hockey's most intense media market. On any given day, Babcock did most of the heavy lifting—in his daily sessions (twice daily on game days), he was good for at least one quotable pronouncement on the Leafs' current state of affairs. The Leafs' dressing room was opened after games and practices, and veteran players were regularly offered up—they were generally approachable, even if they weren't particularly chatty. None were as uncomfortable with reporters as Phil Kessel had been. Access to the rookies, however, was carefully stage-managed. Reporters could ask a few questions—maybe five minutes' worth—and then a media relations staffer intervened, gave his cue for the curtain to drop ("Thanks, Auston"), and escorted the rookies away. Early on, you could see a bit of deer-in-the-headlights in Matthews's expression, though that had eased somewhat by midseason. A media onslaught like the All-Star Game's selling of the stars was exactly what Leafs management had worked hard to avoid.

Lou Lamoriello had never had much time for or trust in the media in New Jersey. It didn't matter if it was a young player or a veteran, there wasn't an interview request that the Devils couldn't decline. New Jersey was the most media-averse organization in the league, and it wasn't like they operated in the spotlight—even when winning Stanley Cups, the team was buried in the back pages of sports sections. What Lamoriello didn't control, he didn't like. He was intensely image conscious, and had been going back to his days in Providence College's athletic department, where he had been equal parts administrator, coach, and father figure.

In the days before the announcement of the All-Star Game rosters, it floated in the Twitter-sphere that Lamoriello would have been just as happy if Matthews didn't go to Los Angeles for the event. It was entirely plausible. It would be no great leap to suggest that Lamoriello would be happy if none of his players went. By scale, the All-Star Game and the speculation about Lou was a small fire, but it was one that management wanted to put out.

Lamoriello went on radio—his preferred medium for getting out his message unfiltered—and explained the team's strategy of managing their young players. The Leafs' approach to handling players made nuclear facilities' handling of radioactive isotopes sound haphazard.

"It's development," Lamoriello said on Sportsnet's radio network. "It's our responsibility to bring them along, to make sure we can take away as many distractions as we can and yet never lose sight of what their responsibility is as a player and what their responsibility is to the media."

Lamoriello went on to suggest that he was actually pleased by the idea of Matthews going to the All-Star Game, that the late January weekend in Los Angeles would be an opportunity to continue Matthews's "learning process and development." Lamoriello is almost certainly the first NHL executive to frame the All-Star weekend in those terms—the entertainment value and players' effort in the contest are virtually nil, and not a few players look at it primarily as a chance to catch up with friends and party. That didn't stop Lamoriello from suggesting that Matthews would benefit from a little time out of the nest and from a weekend with stars whom he'd watched as a kid when they had come in to Phoenix to play the Coyotes.

"He'll be able to see firsthand what the result is of how they handle themselves, how they speak, where the humility is, what affects him," Lamoriello said.

Well, maybe. Maybe Matthews could go to school on Sidney Crosby and Jonathan Toews as they made the rounds, stars whose assiduous avoidance of controversy would have endeared them to

Lamoriello. Then again, Alexander Ovechkin and P. K. Subban were going to be at the game, too. If Matthews returned from Los Angeles a "star," it would cause Lamoriello no end of grief.

Although it might be hard to imagine the septuagenarian Lamoriello changing with the times, there were a few signs he might be a little more flexible than he was in New Jersey. Which is to say, that he'd even be the slightest bit flexible at all. When Lou arrived in Toronto, the presumption was that he'd bring his long-established system of values fully intact. It hadn't quite turned out that way, however. He had never seen a bonus that he liked, yet five days after he came to the Leafs, Lamoriello signed Marner to a rookie contract that included most of what Marner's agent had pushed for. Matthews's negotiations went likewise. Lamoriello had spectacular successes in New Jersey but never had the resources to work with what he'd been given in Toronto. He had some good rookies in his time in New Jersey—one of whom, Martin Brodeur, won the Calder Trophy at age twenty-one. It's fair to say that in his long hockey career, Lou had never had two teenage talents like Matthews and Marner. Things change; maybe Lou could, too.

When Matthews rejoined the Leafs in Boston for a game on Super Bowl weekend in early February, the two teams were nearly deadlocked in the fight for playoff berths in the Eastern Conference. Bruins coach Claude Julien, who had coached Boston to a Stanley Cup in 2011, was in the hot seat. The Leafs loomed large in Julien's sights. A Toronto win in Boston would put them one point behind the Bruins with five games in hand. The optics would be awful for the Bruins coach: his team, a perennial contender with much of its core of Cup winners still in place, would be losing the chase and effectively passed by a perennial doormat with a half-dozen rookies in its line-up. All that said, however, the Leafs were trending in the wrong direction, too. After shutout wins over Calgary at home and the Wings in Detroit, they had lost three consecutive games in regulation for the first time in the season.

By February, it seemed like a pecking order among the Leafs rookies had been established: Matthews followed by Marner followed by Nylander. It came down to these three; the other first-year players—Brown, Hyman, Zaitsev, Soshnikov, and the occasional call-up—were just trying to get into the frame. Matthews was always the first name to drop, but at that point it was Marner—with 42 points, three ahead of Matthews—who was second to Winnipeg's Patrik Laine in rookie scoring. On many nights, it seemed that Marner stole Matthews's thunder, with his flashy dangles and cheeky, almost insolent willingness to take on veterans who towered over him, often undressing them with moves that made NHL games look like shinny contests. Nylander was always the third name to come up, and, with 31 points, he was well behind the others in scoring when the team went to Boston.

Nylander was in a curious position. He had been anointed the saviour when drafted in 2014, heralded as a steal at No. 8 overall. Even on the day of the draft, some had speculated that he might be the most skilled player in his year. The Leafs' drafting Marner the next June and winning Matthews in the lottery had taken the spotlight off Nylander. The team had reset expectations, and Nylander suffered by comparison. Even though he was fourth in rookie scoring overall, a bit of the shine had gone off Nylander over the course of the season.

Matthews and Marner had settled into secure roles in the Leafs' line-up, but Babcock had moved Nylander around. He had started the season on Matthews's line, a good sign early on, but that didn't last. He then seemed to fall out of Mike Babcock's good graces for a while, even as far as the fourth line for a game or two. Many fans and analysts asked hard questions about his game—even when he was being shuffled around, Nylander took regular turns on the Leafs' power play, and his numbers with the unit made his five-on-five stats look very ordinary. In fact, those figures reinforced the questions that had been out there when he was drafted and ever since. His play in Sweden notwithstanding, was Nylander big enough, physical enough to have success in the NHL?

An easy fallback explanation was driven by position. Nylander had played centre at every stage throughout his development, including with the Marlies, but now, with the big club, he had to adapt to playing the wing. He looked lost when the other team had the puck, opponents too often effective on the cycle. Babcock scuttled any questions about moving Nylander to centre as a possible fix. Babcock's refusal to even give him a look at centre came off as a vote of no confidence—maybe if there had been an injury to Matthews, Kadri, or Bozak, Nylander might have been given a shot, not that Babcock ever hinted that he might go that way.

In the run-up to the Boston game, Nylander had only one goal in eight games, giving rise to a school of thought that the youngest Leafs had hit a midseason wall, that they lacked the staying power to allow the team to contend. On the stats sheet, Matthews was slumping as badly as Nylander, with just one goal in seven games. But whenever the press raised questions about Matthews, Babcock was effusive in his praise for the first overall pick's play without the puck, his awareness and positioning in the defensive zone. That he said nothing about Nylander on this count spoke volumes.

But in this pivotal game against Boston, Nylander set out to evoke the not-long-past days when he was touted as the franchise saviour, when ESPN, among others, billed him as the best young prospect not in the NHL.

After the game's early shifts, you were left wondering if Nylander deserved a bigger, more central role. Babcock penciled him in on a line with Kadri and Leo Komarov, the Leafs' two most physical, defensively conscientious of the top-nine forwards. At first glance, it didn't look like a great fit. After an early goal by the Bruins' David Pastrnak opened the scoring in the third minute, Kadri ran defenceman Riley Nash behind the Boston net, setting off a melee, after which he found himself sandwiched between Nash and Matt Beleskey. Torey Krug, a short, squat Boston defenceman, grabbed Nylander as a dancing partner and wrestled with him, and it looked as though the rookie wished he were somewhere, anywhere else.

Midway through the period, the puck finally found Nylander, and Nylander in turn found his game. It occurred while the Leafs were in the middle of a line change. Matthews had just jumped over the boards for Komarov and promptly forced a turnover at the Bruins' blueline, stripping David Backes of the puck. Matthews threw the puck over to Kadri, who skated into open ice on the right wing. Kadri then found Nylander swooping down the far side of the ice, a backhand pass that caught Nylander in full flight, fighting through a hook in vain by Backes. Goaltender Tuukka Rask came out to challenge Nylander at exactly the wrong moment—a slick toe drag past the overcommitted goalie, and Nylander had a wide-open net in front of him, tying the game one-all.

Nylander's goal was just a portent of what was to come.

Nine minutes into the second period, with the Bruins forwards crowding Frederik Andersen, Boston defenceman Kevan Miller lost an edge inside the blueline and Nylander found himself with the puck and 120 feet of open ice ahead of him. He lit out on a two-on-one with Komarov; another Miller—Colin—was the only defenceman to beat. The latter Miller took away the pass and would regret the decision. Nylander cruised right up to the face-off circle, feinted once to get Rask leaning, and then took a step to get a better angle for a wrist shot that he wired into the net on the goalie's glove side. Nylander's second goal of the game put the Leafs out in front 3–1.

A minute later, Nylander was back out on the ice on a power play and completed his hat trick with a hybrid of his first two goals. As it was with the first goal, Matthews stole a puck, this time inside the Boston blueline when it looked like the Bruins were going to clear the zone. This time the middleman was Connor Brown, who hit Nylander on the far side of the ice, standing in almost exactly the same spot where he had scored on the two-on-one. Nylander had the luxury of time—Zdeno Chara was the nearest defender, but he was a couple of stick lengths away. Unlike many young players, Nylander didn't rush, and he almost kept Rask hanging before snapping the puck past him.

After the goal, Claude Julien pulled the former Vezina winner. In the meantime, the Leafs media relations staff was sent scrambling. With Matthews' four-goal game against Ottawa and Nylander's three in Boston, the Leafs had two rookies score hat tricks in the same season for the first time in ninety years. When Ace Bailey and Bill Carson recorded their hat tricks back in 1926–27, the Toronto franchise was still known as the St. Pats.

In a season that hadn't lacked for games with massive swings, the game in Boston might have been the most frantic. The Bruins roared back to tie the game at 4–4. Connor Brown gave the Leafs a 5–4 lead with less than five minutes left, but again the home team tied it up. It took a late goal by James van Riemsdyk, his second of the game, to give the Leafs the victory.

The Leafs' rookies couldn't rid themselves of doubts about their ability to stand up across a long NHL season, but collectively, this might have been their biggest win of the season: four goals and seven assists, three of them from Matthews. Still, for this night at least, the spotlight wasn't on Matthews but on the onetime franchise saviour who seemed at risk of being relegated in the mix.

Nylander first appeared on Toronto's radar at NHL Central Scouting's combine in the city back in the spring of 2014. He was a player of interest, a guaranteed first-rounder, the second-ranked European player on Central Scouting's list. He had lived up to that billing at the world under-18 championships weeks earlier when he led the tournament in scoring. He was also a compelling story. His father, Michael, not only had played more than nine hundred games in the league with six NHL teams but also played with his son on Rogle in the Swedish Elite League that season. And even if you didn't know him by name or by reputation, even if you didn't care about hockey at all, William Nylander got everyone's attention whenever he walked into a room—with his self-assured sense of presence and a head of hair that borrowed equally from Prince Valiant and the boy band of your choice, he had to be *somebody*. The top-ranked European player in that draft class, Kasperi Kapanen, noted, "Girls want their photo with him. We just hold the camera."

Even without the pedigree and the look, the younger Nylander would have gained attention with his play as a junior. At sixteen, he played a handful of games against proven pros with Sodertalje in the SEL. The year he became a full-time pro, splitting the season between Sodertalje, Modo, and Rogle, he scored 16 goals in fifty-seven games. He had no holes in his skill set; he was elite in every facet of the offensive game. There was only one red flag, and it was one that he had no control over: his father.

In his long NHL career, Michael Nylander had crossed paths with many of the NHL executives and scouts who were evaluating his son, and Michael Nylander hadn't made a great impression on many of them. In the opinion of one NHL scout who had played with him, "He was a talented guy but a me-first type, selfish. He wasn't a coach killer, but he wasn't committed to the team concept. If he gets his goals, gets his contract . . . whatever he can get out of it."

Another who played with Michael called him "the worst teammate I ever had . . . it was always all about him."

That Michael played for himself was a common view. Not that he was poison in the dressing room—it was just that he wasn't what guys thought of as a good soldier, not even a soldier for hire, or a teammate first.

Some in hockey were tempted to paint William with the same brush. Could the apple fall far from the tree? they wondered. Some others who were ready to give William a fairer shake would admit to concerns about his father's influence. Teams like to have a player's complete attention and not compete with a parent or agent or anyone else who might offer a second opinion.

William Nylander impressed everyone who watched him in physical testing at the combine. "A pure athlete who wasn't even physically mature yet, lots of room for growth," said one NHL team's director of scouting. Check marks beside: height (a half inch under six feet); power (second in a group of more than one hundred players in anaerobic testing); lower-body squat strength (in the ninetieth percentile in the test group); and fitness (up in the eightieth percentile). Scouts didn't worry too much that he weighed only 172 pounds, 17 less than the average prospect, because they saw that he had the frame to pack on more useful weight and gain more strength. Nylander managed only one rep on the bench press, but that was really comic relief for the scouts looking on. He already had a heavy shot, pro quality, and if he were to gain strength, it would become that much heavier. The bottom line: He wasn't yet physically ready to step into the NHL, not at eighteen, but scouts could easily project him there in a season or two.

Prospects' interviews with teams are a mixed bag—no young player has talked his way onto a club, although a few have hurt their chances when talking with teams. Everything is open to interpretation and scouts' predispositions. Scouts have a unique talent for talking themselves into supposedly character-challenged players and out of reputed Boy Scouts. William Nylander's interviews were a priority for teams with picks in the top fifteen at the draft, mostly because of their views of his father.

One scout who gave Nylander high grades based on performance came away from the combine pegging him as aloof and "really full of himself." The scout mentioned that he spotted Nylander wearing jeans and sneakers but no shirt and walking with a bunch of prospects over to a restaurant down the street from the hotel, stuff that passes for rock stars but not NHL players.

Another scout who knew Michael was willing to give both son and father the benefit of the doubt.

"He was pretty much the kid I thought he would be. He grew up around NHL arenas, so he knows the drill. Polite, considered his answers, didn't tell you what he thought you wanted to hear. Talking to him, I didn't get the idea that he was aware of his father's reputation around the league. I asked him if he liked the game—you know, it's a problem if a kid is just doing it because his father pushed him into it. That wasn't the case, though. I thought he was pretty genuine about loving the game and just being around the arena. At the end of the day, you have to say that maybe [Michael] was a pain in the ass, but that doesn't mean he doesn't have his kid's best interests in mind."

The Leafs weren't going to tip their hand about their interview with William Nylander. Back in 2014, the head of their amateur scouting department was Dave Morrison, a man who had overseen the Leafs' drafts for a decade and had taken a lot of criticism from fans. Under his direction, the Leafs' scouting team made at least a couple of home-run picks—Tuukka Rask and Alexander Steen—who were traded away for laughable returns. In the 2006 draft, the Leafs selected seven players, and six of them went on to play more than one hundred games in the NHL, including Leo Komarov, taken in the sixth round, 180th overall. And the Leafs' worst recent pick was one that Morrison had been overruled on by then-GM Brian Burke—the team had traded two second-round picks to move up to No. 21 in the first round and select Tyler Biggs, a forward who, after he was drafted, was a frequent healthy scratch with the Marlies, was sent along to Pittsburgh in the Kessel trade, and seemed likely never to play an NHL game.

In the 2014 NHL draft, Morrison was free of Burke, but he might not have had an entirely free hand. But he did still plan for the Leafs to take "a big swing" at the draft.

The Leafs never would have called William Nylander's name if Brian Burke had stuck around. But whatever the Leafs management thought about Michael Nylander's perceived issues clearly paled in comparison to his son's skill, and the Leafs selected William with the eighth overall draft pick. Fans and the media viewed it as a clean break, a shift from the franchise paradigm under Brian Burke. They still didn't mind hyping the selection, mind you—a seeming carryover from Burke claiming that Morgan Rielly was the top-ranked player of his draft class in the Leafs' books. "[Nylander] might be the most skilled player in the draft," GM Dave Nonis said.

Not that he was walking back his estimation, but in the next breath Nonis made it sound highly unlikely that Nylander was going to line up with the big club that season. "He'll get a chance to show us what he can do in training camp," he said.

You could read into Nonis's demeanor that, at some level, he knew that Nylander's future with the Leafs was going to be brighter and longer-lived than his own.

Those who had closely tracked Nylander's progress in the organization might have drawn parallels between the hat-trick game in Boston and the first time he skated in a Leafs sweater, a preseason rookie game against the Chicago Blackhawks freshmen back in the fall of 2014.

Rookie games, which take place before the veterans even report to training camp, usually don't merit much attention, but this contest was another matter simply because of Nylander, the first first-round pick in Shanahan's administration. The entire Toronto media horde made it out to London, where the team was hosting a four-team rookie tournament, and the game was featured on Leafs TV, the team's in-house network. It was virtually blanket coverage, and Nylander didn't disappoint. At a morning practice before the game, he came off as matter-of-fact, rather than brash, about his intentions in training camp.

"I'm always aiming as high as possible," he said. "I want to take a spot on the roster [of the NHL club] and maybe play a game or a couple of games." He wasn't in denial about the reality of the situation, however. Success wasn't going to be sticking with the club for eighty-two games that season. That wasn't going to be in the cards at all. Success was going to be showing that he could have an impact in games, that he was able to create chances and finish them with the puck on his stick.

It took barely twenty minutes for Nylander's talent to shine through. While he was the youngest player on the ice, Nylander wasn't playing "up"—in fact, it looked as though he was playing against a level of competition at least a full step down from what he was accustomed to in the Swedish Elite League. He caught everyone's eye on his very first shift as he created a turnover at the Chicago blueline and wound up with a shot in the slot, forcing a scrambling save by Blackhawks goaltender Mac Carruth. On his second shift, he created an even better scoring chance, carrying the puck up the ice on a two-on-one—much like his second goal in the hat trick against the Bruins—but he rushed his shot, even as he was pulling away from the defenders chasing him. A couple of shifts later, he completely hoodwinked a pair of young Chicago defencemen, played them for suckers, and slipped behind them for a clean breakaway. Carruth was equal to him yet again, but barely ten minutes into the game, Nylander had both a potential hat trick and a hat trick of potential—an educated stick, speed, and hockey sense. The game was cautious and scoreless and the puck was mostly bogged down in the neutral zone, but the Leafs rookies had three scoring chances, and Nylander was in the middle of all of them.

Nylander didn't score in the game—Carruth denied him two or three more times. Still, the Leafs beat the Hawks 4–2, and Nylander did pick up an assist on a goal by David Broll, a long, cross-ice pass onto the tape of Broll's stick on a two-on-one. He could have had a couple more assists if his green teammates had been ready for his passes through traffic—everyday stuff that an experienced Swedish Elite League player would handle and bury.

After the game, the Leafs' rookie team's coach—Gord Dineen, the Marlies' head man—expressed excitement about Nylander's ability with the puck, but he suggested his game without the puck was much more a work in progress. "Any kid who can skate like that and has his skill set . . . We feel he has got offence and can also play a great two-way game. In Europe, that [offence] was what they were looking for. Over here, we're looking for a two-way game, and I've cited some examples of [NHL players] he could strive to be."

Dineen's evaluation of Nylander's game had merit, but it also revealed how hard it was going to be to shake old stereotypes. What Dineen posited as a hole in Nylander's game, which was somehow tied to being a European, was a jab, and a goofy one at that. Virtually all teenage pro prospects have to figure out the southbound game—they have forever had the puck and been headed due north, dominating play growing up. And, yes, they focused on the "fun" aspect of the game rather than the drudgery of back-checking. But more than that, those who knew Nylander best would have told you that, heritage aside, he really wasn't a European player at all.

"I saw Williams's name on the European scouting list and I thought it was strange in a way, because to me, he is a North American player . . . or a hybrid, maybe," Anders Sorensen said. "Maybe it's that he looks like a Swede. But as a coach, to me I see his shot . . . and I see his quick stick. . . .When I see that, that's the North American game."

Sorensen's perspective is informed by experience: he has likely spent more time working on the ice with William Nylander and his younger brother, Alexander, than anyone except their father. He worked with the Nylanders on two continents, and even coached Michael for a season.

A former pro with his hometown team, Sodertalje, Sorensen spent a few seasons in the North American minor leagues and was only a couple of years out of the game when he took a job as a coach with the Chicago Mission. Not long after, Michael Nylander, who was playing for the Blackhawks, brought in William to skate in the atom program at Mission, likely the biggest youth hockey organization in the Midwest. "At seven or eight, William was clearly very advanced compared to the other boys a year or two older than him," Sorensen said. "Physically, he could use his edges to get away from players, a superior skater. What was really impressive, though, was his understanding of the game. He thought the game so well, better than some of the fourteen-year-olds."

When Michael moved on to play for the Washington Capitals, his family went with him, and the Nylander boys had to find other programs closer to their new, temporary home. Still, Michael stayed in touch with Sorensen, and when William was fourteen, his family moved back to Chicago, and the Nylander boys once again enrolled in the Mission program. Michael lined up beside Christian Dvorak and Nick Schmaltz, two future NHL draft picks, and the Mission team competed with the elite bantam teams on the North American circuit. "The '96's was a really strong year," Sorensen said. "We were in there against the Marlies, who had Connor McDavid, and Belle Tire in Detroit, who had Dylan Larkin."

"I remember when we went into Detroit to play Belle Tire and we got a four–four tie, and Willie got all four goals," said Christian Dvorak. "It was a crazy game. A couple of times out there I thought, *Did you really just do that?*"

Sorensen said that William was a perfect running mate for Dvorak and Schmaltz. "Sometimes a talented kid doesn't play well with others or wants to do things all by himself, but that wasn't William at all," he said. "On the ice he was a creative guy, but he created for the other kids on his line as much as himself. He liked to throw the puck around. He wasn't selfish, but he wouldn't pass up a good chance."

William's success as a bantam came despite physical disadvantages. On a physical maturity curve, he lagged behind most of the elite kids. "William was always athletic and he was strong for his size, but he was shorter and skinny," said Sorensen. "At fourteen, you'd see other kids who were becoming young men, and Willie was really a boy. He wasn't physically dominating like some of the other players in his year, and you could see that as good as he was, he had a ceiling that they didn't."

After William's bantam year and Alexander's peewee season, and after Michael's NHL career had run its course, the Nylanders moved back to Sweden. In time, Sorensen would follow them, and a couple of years later he was behind the bench coaching Michael, at age forty, and his linemate, William, then seventeen. "It was comical a lot of the time," Sorensen said. "They were more like brothers than father and son. After a shift they would get back to the bench and they would get under each other's skin. . . . 'You didn't pass to me. Give me the puck.' Either one would say the same thing."

In William's first pro game, against Leksand, after getting called up from the under-18 team, Michael could have taken his digs at his son for not passing to him. The teenager picked up his first professional point at the end of a sequence that would be familiar to those who tracked his game in his rookie season with the Leafs. William skated around the perimeter in Leksand's end, effectively taking a lap, surveying the scene and looking for an open man. Michael seemed to be open and looked to his son, who looked elsewhere, passing to defenceman Johan Jonsson, who fired the puck into the net.

On plays like that, NHL scouts could see the skills that William possessed, but many still couldn't get past the idea of the son playing with the father, especially the notion that Michael somehow used his clout to get William into the line-up or to bring in Sorensen to coach. As much as the scouts could understand the draw of a veteran's chance to play with his son, they were put off, assuming Michael had made it happen. Sorensen disagreed. "William was there on merit," he said.

William Nylander went back to Sweden at the end of his first Leafs training camp, but he didn't play with his father in Sodertalje. The Mississauga Steelheads of the OHL had selected William in the CHL import draft, thinking that playing in the Leafs' backyard would have been attractive to both the prospect and the big club. It was an idea that was dead on arrival—the CHL would have been a significant step back from the SEL, and the notion that William needed time to adapt to the North American game ignored the fact that he grew up playing on eighty-by-two-hundred-foot sheets.

When William returned to Sweden, he landed with Modo, a famous program, albeit one in a down cycle. It was a new team, new teammates, no special favour or consideration. Because Modo missed the playoffs, Nylander was able to come back to Toronto in mid-March and join the Marlies. He finished the 2014–15 season with the AHL affiliate, and the Leafs were categorical about their development plan for him: a slow build, season-long if necessary, with the carrot that a late season call-up was out there if he progressed as they hoped. And those scouts and executives who voiced concerns about Michael's (over-)involvement in his son's career had to have been amused but not surprised when they heard that he was coming over to Toronto when William was destined for the Marlies at the start of the 2015 season. Michael took a job as an assistant coach with the Steelheads, where he could oversee Alexander, playing with the OHL club in his draft year, all the while keeping tabs on William.

The standard line for William was that he needed to physically fill out to be able to stand up to the wear and tear in the NHL, and there was some truth to that. It wasn't just a maturing body, though;

there was also the need for emotional growth. He had grown up around NHL teams and hung out in NHL dressing rooms, but always as the veteran's son. With the Marlies, he thrived right off the hop. Whether he succeeded or failed, William's future was about to become all his own.

CHAPTER NINE

THOUGH THE LEAFS HAD SURGED IN MIDSEASON, EVEN WHEN playing their best hockey, they consistently struggled with back-to-back games, or at least the second game in consecutive nights. It would be expected of most NHL teams, especially of one with so many young players, those who are learning about the NHL grind and are not yet physically up to the challenge. By mid-February, the numbers made a powerful case: an impressive 9-2-2 in the first of such two-game series, they were only 4-8-1 in the back half.

So, it wasn't surprising that the Leafs beat the Islanders at the ACC on February 14 and lost to Columbus the next night. But the divide between the games was striking. At home, the Leafs rolled over the Islanders 7–1, a desperately needed win over another team in the chase for a wild-card spot in the Eastern Conference. The Blue Jackets figured to be a stiffer challenge wherever they fell in a schedule—for a long stretch of the midseason, they were the NHL's hottest club, and they played with a physical edge that caused problems for Toronto's skill up front. It didn't seem like the outcome was ever in doubt: a bad match-up plus bad timing equaled a 5–2 loss in Columbus, a loss that felt more one-sided than the score suggested. A split wasn't the worst news, however. A far greater concern was a shoulder injury that knocked Mitch Marner out of the game.

It wasn't the biggest hit in the NHL that night. Columbus centre Boone Jenner wouldn't be accused of running Marner, who was

likely giving away forty pounds in the match-up. It seemed like almost an incidental collision in the neutral zone, but when players are
moving even at cruising speed, incidental collisions have outsized
consequences. With the Leafs down 4–0 late in the second period,
Jenner brushed Marner's left shoulder, which knocked Marner flying
into the boards without time to brace himself. It could have had a far
worse result—he was turned around just enough to avoid going into
the wall headfirst. Still, it looked ugly.

Marner managed to get up and skate over to the bench. He
winced and ducked his head. He went down the hallway to the
Leafs' dressing room to get examined and, at two later junctures,
took shifts in the game. On the latter, early in the third period, after
almost slipping the puck past goaltender Joonas Korpisalo, Marner
tried to duck under towering defenceman Seth Jones, and just the
slightest, unintended contact made Marner's knees buckle. He was
done for the game. The fear was that Marner, the Leafs' leading
scorer with 48 points in fifty-six games at that point, might have suffered a fractured collarbone or a shoulder dislocation. It wound up
being a sprain, one that would keep him out of the line-up for a couple of weeks. More of a scare than a knockout blow to their hopes of
making the playoffs.

While Marner and his injury were the focus of attention in Columbus, a couple of turns in the game went largely unnoticed. For
one, the veterans on Marner's line, James van Riemsdyk and Tyler
Bozak, were left on the bench in the third period by Mike Babcock.
The coach stopped short of calling the pair out by name, saying simply in a *Toronto Star* interview, "When we don't play hard enough,
I address it." It was almost certainly just a coincidence that their
names were at the top of the list of those tossed around in rumours
leading up to the trading deadline—if you didn't think much of
the Leafs' chances of making the playoffs and had eyes only on the

future, you might think that you could convert van Riemsdyk into a pick or a prospect, or that some team would be interested in adding depth down the middle with Bozak and his cap-friendly contract expiring after the 2017–18 season. It was easy to read too much into the two veterans sitting out shifts in the late going of a sure loss.

Arguably Toronto's best player on that lousy night was Josh Leivo, a call-up from the Marlies. The Leafs' AHL affiliate mostly flies under the media radar in an achingly self-described "world-class city," although the Marlies did achieve some profile in the NHL club's 2015–16 tank season. While the parent club was deeply committed to a thorough teardown, the Marlies finished first in the North Division with 54 wins in seventy-six games—their 114 points were the league's best by a dozen. Although they were knocked out of the playoffs in the third round, that Marlies team featured emerging players who would go on to be fixtures among the forwards in the Leafs' line-up this season: William Nylander, Zach Hyman, and Connor Brown.

Other Marlies would get called up for stretches—Nikita Soshnikov didn't start the season in the big club's line-up, but his grinding style earned him a regular spot on the fourth line a few weeks in. Soshnikov moved up the organizational board at the expense of Leivo, among others. The knock on Leivo was that he didn't have enough jam to be a fourth-liner. Though he didn't look to the "energy" or "grinding" line that much, Babcock preferred Soshnikov beside centre Ben Smith and veteran tough guy Matt Martin. Still, Leivo did manage to pick up a goal against the Islanders and said that he "was getting more comfortable" in the Leafs' line-up.

While Matthews, Marner, and Nylander played in the spotlight, the internal competition in the Marlies organization—literally a cab ride away from the ACC, at the Ricoh Coliseum—was a fascinating one. The Marlies didn't just provide easy access to fill holes that opened in the line-up due to injury. They were an ever-present reminder that no one should get too comfortable.

When Shanahan arrived in Toronto, the Marlies had been an afterthought for Leafs management for more than a decade. The last Leafs team to feel the warm embrace of Toronto fans had been the one that bridged the last century and the new millennium, coached and managed by Pat Quinn, led by Mats Sundin, and featuring a cast of characters that included Gary Roberts, Shayne Corson, Tie Domi, and Darcy Tucker. Since that time, the Maple Leafs had been built more through trade and free agency than drafting and development. The last Toronto team before the lockout featured only three players who had put in any significant time with the AHL affiliate (which was then based in St. John's, Newfoundland): Nik Antropov, Alexei Ponikarovsky, and Karel Pilar. Effectively, St. John's had been just the Leafs' way station for drafted prospects brought over from Europe for a season of orientation. The roster of the Leafs team under Brian Burke didn't even feature that many AHL graduates, and there was only one in a significant role: Nazem Kadri. In Burke's time, the AHL had become a repository of bad contracts, where bad decisions were buried: mercurial forward Tim Connolly spent a season with the Marlies, the second year of a two-year, $9.5 million contract that Brian Burke signed him to. And another of Burke's free agent signings, defenceman Mike Komisarek, spent a season making $4.5 million with the Marlies before the team could exercise a buyout of his contract.

Brendan Shanahan played for five NHL clubs, but he is best remembered for his time with the Detroit Red Wings, a stint that lasted nine seasons across the prime of his career and allowed him to raise the Stanley Cup three times. Fans hoped that Shanahan would be able to adopt the Wings' team-building strategy in the front office; that he could graft Detroit's winning culture and allow it to grow in the Leafs organization. To an extent, this was wishful thinking. Shanahan had last donned a Detroit sweater in 2006, and the way in which the Red Wings had built the rosters of their Stanley Cup–winning teams had long ago become untenable in the NHL when MLSE hired Shanahan in 2014.

When Detroit was winning the Cup in Shanahan's time there, the Red Wings' owner, Mike Ilitch, dug deeper into his pockets than almost anybody else in the NHL. They were the most consistent winners in a fundamentally different league, one that was divided into haves and have-nots. The Wings, counting themselves among the haves, could take on unlimited salary, and did. Their willingness to spend lavishly on talent made Detroit the most popular destination in the league. Veterans wanted to stay there, and free agents wanted to go there.

The Wings, however, had to change their ways when the owners stared down the NHLPA and canceled the 2004–5 season. That lockout led to a collective agreement that put into place a cap on team payrolls. There would be no more going to the market and simply buying talent or trading for veterans with ugly contracts. When the salary cap was established, the conventional wisdom held that no team would be hurt as severely as Detroit. But within three seasons, the team had won the Cup again, and they would make the playoffs for eleven straight seasons with the cap in place.

It seemed, then, that Shanahan borrowed from the Red Wings not the team of his glory years but rather the iteration that he left, a franchise that somehow found continued success in the new system.

Going back to the 1980s and '90s, the Wings had arguably the sharpest scouting staff in the league, mining all-star talents like Nicklas Lidstrom in the middle rounds of the draft and Pavel

Datsyuk after other teams had packed up and left the building. Detroit GM Ken Holland put a heavy emphasis on his minor-league system—that is, in exercising patience in developing drafted players. Other organizations would rush eighteen-year-olds into the NHL line-up before they were ready; there are too many in Leafs history to list, but one of the most painful recent examples was throwing teenager Luke Schenn out on the blueline during Brian Burke's regime. The first Wings team that won the Cup two seasons after Shanahan's departure provides the instructive example: Jiri Hudler, Valtteri Filppula, and Darren Helm, among others, were all recent grads of Detroit's AHL affiliate in Grand Rapids, Michigan. The idea was that extensive grooming at the AHL level spared teaching young pros at the highest level of the game—if they were going to learn from making mistakes in games, let it be in the minors, where it was better for them and also better for the veterans with the big club.

If anything, Detroit's model in the salary cap era borrowed largely from the first stop on Shanahan's journey, New Jersey, the team that drafted him second overall out of London in 1987. The GM who called out Shanahan's name at the draft, Lou Lamoriello, established a clear and rigid hierarchy when he was at the helm of the Devils: No player moved up the chain before his time. Shanahan was an exception—he scored 22 goals at nineteen, then 30 at age twenty. More typical were players such as Jim Dowd, a player who had his name engraved on the Stanley Cup but was returned to the AHL for further grooming after the fact. As in Detroit, the object lesson was plain: The work doesn't end with the draft.

The Leafs' 2016–17 line-up was a good measure of the priority that management had brought to Toronto's internal development. Nylander, Brown, Hyman, and Soshnikov were all products of the Marlies, as were occasional call-ups Frédérik Gauthier, Antoine Bibeau, and Josh Leivo. Yes, the AHL was still a place to hide bad contracts, but those were in fact players that Leafs management had traded for: Toronto had taken Brooks Laich and his $4.5 million-a-year contract off Washington's hands; likewise the team had taken Colin Greening from Ottawa after the Senators had signed him to a $2 million per year deal, only to see his game fall off immediately thereafter. In contrast to past management, which tendered burdensome deals, the Leafs helped out teams unwilling or unable to exercise buyouts and in need of salary cap relief.

Veterans such as Laich and Greening, however, were exceptions on the 2016–17 Marlies team. Most players were more likely to benefit from an apprenticeship in the AHL—players such as Kasperi Kapanen, who was in his second season with the Marlies.

Kapanen had been the most significant return from the trade that sent Phil Kessel to the Pittsburgh Penguins. Like Nylander, Kapanen had been a member of the 2014 draft class. In fact, NHL Central Scouting had rated Kapanen as the top European prospect in that draft year, with Nylander one slot below him.

And like Nylander, Kapanen didn't lack confidence. When called in by teams at the combine, he told them that he had a clear idea of his role: "Pure scorer." He tempered his self-evaluation when talking to the media, saying that there were aspects of the game that he would have to work on, that he was going to put in a full summer of hard training. Still, his confidence crossed over into moral certainty that he was going to be a player at the next level sooner rather than later.

And, yes, like Nylander, Kapanen was not only the North American–born son of a European NHLer but also played in his draft year on a line beside his father. In Kapanen's case, he played beside his forty-year-old father, Sami, on a line with KalPa Kuopio, a Finnish league team. "We gave it to each other," Kasperi said. "I'm telling him, 'Give me the puck.'"

Just as with Nylander, scouts couldn't help but recall the father Kapanen when looking at the son. While this probably did few favours for Nylander, it wouldn't have hurt Kapanen at all—in many ways, Sami Kapanen could be perceived as a counterpoint to Michael Nylander. A consistent 20-goal scorer in his prime years, the elder Kapanen won universal respect around the league for his speed and work ethic. He had one run to the Stanley Cup final in 2002, when Carolina was routed by a Detroit team featuring Brendan Shanahan. Perhaps Kapanen's defining moment was an unfortunate one, but it displayed his character and toughness. In overtime of Game 6 in the second round of the 2004 playoffs, Kapanen, playing for the Philadelphia Flyers, was drilled into the glass by the Leafs' Darcy Tucker, knocked completely airborne and clearly concussed on the play. The scene was frightening: Kapanen trying three times to get back up on his skates to get to the bench, only to fall and flail while play moved back up the ice into the Leafs' end; at one point, his teammate Keith Primeau opened the Flyers' gate, extended his stick, and tried to pull the dazed Kapanen off the ice. Kapanen had barely sat down, when Jeremy Roenick scored the series-winning goal. Kasperi was weeks away from his eighth birthday when he watched the scene play out on television. He told Leafs TV, "I've seen it once, and I never want to watch it again. It's not fun seeing your dad in that condition, but I'm really proud of him getting up and skating to the bench, because [Roenick] scored the goal fifteen seconds later. It was a tough spot for me to see him coming home not in the best shape of his life, and it made me mad at Darcy and the Leafs, but that's the past."

The Penguins wound up selecting Kapanen with the twenty-second pick in the 2015 draft, and he had an impressive training camp with Pittsburgh, even threatening to start the season with the big club as an eighteen-year-old. He didn't make the cut, though, and so Kapanen headed back to Finland to play in Kuopio. He struggled somewhat in Europe, but the Penguins brought him back at the end of the Finnish league season to put in a few games with their AHL affiliate in Wilkes-Barre, Pennsylvania, where Kapanen enjoyed immediate success—he scored on his second AHL shift, and led the team on a run to the playoffs. He had no idea that those would be the last games he'd play for the Pittsburgh organization.

When Kapanen came over to the Maple Leafs organization in 2015, he had a clear understanding of the season that lay ahead of him. Like the other top Leafs prospects, he would spend most of the season with the Marlies; like Nylander, he'd be loaned out to his national under-20 team for the World Junior Championships in Helsinki. And, if he showed enough upside, he might be looking at a late-season call-up to the big club for a sample of the big time.

But Kapanen's time with the Marlies was a disappointment to him. When the farm club's season started, he came down with a crushing case of the flu and lost the better of ten pounds. When he returned to the line-up, he had trouble scoring, struggled to earn ice time, and fell down the pecking order of prospects. Then he suffered a back injury that put him on the sidelines. Going home to play for Finland at the world juniors wasn't a done deal for him, especially given his sluggish return from illness. "That's something we're going to talk about with [management]," Kapanen said. "It's still something that intrigues me. It's back home in Finland, so I would be excited about that. Other than that, I really can't say anything about it."

The Leafs eventually gave the okay to both Nylander and Kapanen to join their respective national teams at the 2016 world juniors. Nylander, the dominant player in the AHL, lasted but a handful of shifts before being knocked out of the tournament. The return to Finland didn't exactly raise Kapanen's game—expected to be a leading scorer for the team, he wound up being just a support player. In the end, however, he did have the ultimate moment of glory, scoring the golden goal, the overtime winner against Russia in the final. And in the dressing room, Kapanen danced a goofy jig that went viral online. It looked like he had turned his season and his fortunes in the organization around. He hadn't.

On February 29, 2016—the season before Matthews came to town—the Leafs provided a glimpse of their future with a call-up of Nylander, Hyman, Soshnikov, and Kapanen. Even though Nylander had sat out significant time with the concussion he suffered in Finland, he had played five more AHL games than Kapanen, who had struggled to keep step. Nylander would hang around with the Leafs until the season's end, playing in twenty-two games and picking up six goals and seven assists before rejoining the Marlies for the playoffs. Hyman and Soshnikov established that they had games that could fill roles on third or fourth lines. Kapanen, alone among them, struggled. He showed more than decent skating ability. Still, he looked as though he had lost his compass on occasional shifts, and he was the first of the four to be returned to the AHL after not registering a point in eight games. Back with the Marlies for the playoffs, it was more of the same—Kapanen was down the list of prospects. He needed a reboot.

It seemed as though things were finally coming together across the first three months of the 2017 season, when Kapanen led the Marlies in scoring. Once again, though, the Leafs summoned other Marlies to the big club before him, calling up Soshnikov and Leivo early in the season. Waiting his turn and scoring a point a game, Kapanen went down with an injury in mid-January—Syracuse defenceman Jake Dotchin got his knee and put Kapanen on crutches until March. It wasn't clear if Kapanen was going to return at all, especially after the Leafs called up Leivo and he picked up 10 points in thirteen games. It looked like yet another prospect was moving up the chain at Kapanen's expense. "It's frustrating, but you just have to keep working, doing what you're doing, and hope one day it all comes together," Kapanen would later say about his injury. He could have easily been describing his nearly two full seasons with the Marlies.

When Kapanen joined the Marlies at the start of the 2015–16 season, he struck up a fast and predictable friendship with Nylander. They had much in common: first-round draft picks who, as kids, kicked around their fathers' NHL dressing rooms; culturally, they were more citizens of hockey than of either North America, where they'd spent so many years, or their families' Scandinavian home-lands. Back in the fall of 2016, they were playing for different teams in the same city. In the new year, while one was on the sidelines with the farm team, the other was breaking through with the big club. It seemed their paths were heading in entirely different directions. It wouldn't be long, though, before they would converge once again.

Marner's absence while recovering from his shoulder injury would require some line shuffling, so Connor Brown was moved up to play beside Tyler Bozak and James van Riemsdyk. At some level, it might have seemed like a downgrade for Bozak and JVR. With Marner gone, all that puck-handling flash and dazzle, that ability to undress defenders with sleight of hand and stick, was lost, and in its place was a player who stood out in no obvious way. Brown skated well but would lose a footrace to a lot of players in the Leafs' line-up. He couldn't fire the puck like Matthews and Nylander. He wasn't quite average size for the league. That's not to say that he didn't stand out in any way, though. Of all the Leafs' rookies, Brown's game was the subtlest, in some ways the most rewarding to track. He squeezed the most out of every opportunity, more with hockey sense and guile than with pure athleticism.

The most instructive example was a contest in Carolina just a few days after Marner's injury against Columbus, in what turned out to be Brown's second two-goal game of the season. The Leafs had staggered through the first period, outplayed by the Hurricanes, outshot 17–9, and lucky that the game was still scoreless. A couple of shifts after intermission, Brown was cruising up ice in the neutral zone while van Riemsdyk was carrying the puck down the left wing. Brown anticipated van Riemsdyk pulling up in front of a Hurricanes defenceman, and he timed a burst to hit the blueline at top speed, flashing down the middle of the ice. Brown charted a course that put himself between JVR and the Carolina blueliner on the far side, Noah Hanifin (who happened to be the player selected after Marner in the 2015 draft).

Hanifin was a physical specimen, a horse, and in a straight race would beat Brown if the latter had been easing up at the line. In four strides, though, Brown blew by Hanifin, crossing into the Hurricanes' zone—a matter of timing and reading of play. Hanifin was overcommitted, too far up from the blueline and leaning in the wrong direction. A right-handed shot, Brown kept himself in an open-body position, turned at 45 degrees to give van Riemsdyk a clear target and to prevent Hanifin from wrapping around and reaching Brown's stick. Having sealed off the defender, Brown laid the blade of his stick on the ice for van Riemsdyk to hit. The pass into the middle was almost true. It saucered and bounced twice, but Brown caught it on the skip-up. He deftly deflected it, jabbing at the puck with the open face of his blade so that it went high and into the top corner past goaltender Cam Ward.

The goal wasn't exactly Connor Brown making something out of nothing—there was an opportunity there, but he had started to capitalize on it a hundred feet away from the Carolina goal, seeing a lane open up from the other side of centre a full four seconds before the puck would hit his stick. It was Brown's play without the puck that made the goal. Babcock and Sheldon Keefe, who coached Brown with the Marlies, always cited Brown's vision as the one aspect of his game that was especially advanced for a young player. It's a facet of a young player's game that was easy to miss, of course. Easy to miss, too, was Connor Brown.

First impressions sometimes lie, and the first impression of Connor Brown on the ice was . . . well, you could be excused if you missed him. It was early September 2013, and he was in a training camp scrimmage at Mercyhurst College—there were more than a few players on the ice trying out for major junior and bound to get sent down. The rink left something to be desired. The ice wasn't even flat—in one corner you had to skate uphill to fetch a dump-in. Connor Brown blended into the background in that scrimmage, but then again, so did everyone, because the foreground was occupied by the player everyone had shown up to interview: Connor McDavid. Brown, nineteen at the time, was skating with the sixteen-year-old that everyone in hockey was talking about.

"Every day, he does something that just leaves you shaking your head," Brown said of McDavid.

Surprisingly, Sherry Bassin, who was then the owner of the Erie Otters, talked almost equally about McDavid and Brown. Brown had been a sixth-round pick of the Leafs, 156th overall in 2012, the range in the draft of long shots, afterthoughts, and those destined to be career minor leaguers. The call on the pick was made by Dave Morrison, then the head of the Leafs' amateur scouting department, who was based in London. The Leafs and a couple of other teams had talked to Brown and his family, but there wasn't any major clamour for the young player.

"Honestly, I had seen him a couple of times and really never thought about him as a prospect," said one veteran NHL scout. "Dave saw something I don't know that anyone would have."

A fair number of players selected around Brown didn't even get tendered contracts by the teams that drafted them—teams would wait out the two-year signing period and take a good, hard look to see if the player was panning out enough to justify the time, bother, and minimal investment.

In his draft year, Brown had been listed at five foot eleven and 160 pounds, and, a year later, looked not as tall as that.

"This kid [Brown] is just a great little player," Bassin said. "I honestly think that he's going to make it. I took him in the thirteenth round [251st overall in the OHL draft] but I didn't know if he could play in this league. . . . I had seen him because I was looking at other kids on that team—a defenceman I took in the first round, Adam Pelech, and a couple of other kids. I kept coming back to Connor. His father, Dan, coached him there, and he was like a coach's son as a player—team in front of anything individual. . . . When he made the team, I thought, *Okay, that's a heck of a run you've had, enjoy it . . .* y'know, a kid who'd just be happy to be on the team, and he goes out and scores twenty-seven goals, leads the team in scoring. Just when you think the kid hits a ceiling, he goes right through it."

Although Brown had 27 goals that season, the team won just ten games all year, and along the way, he went a mind-boggling minus-72. If you had walked up to anyone at Mercyhurst and told them that one of the players on the ice would lead the OHL in scoring that season, no one would have doubted you for a second—they just would have assumed you were talking about Connor McDavid, not the other Connor. But that season, Connor Brown racked up 45 goals and 128 points, winning honours as the OHL Player of the Year. And yet, still people didn't credit Brown—many put it down to him having an opportunity to play with McDavid. They still didn't want to believe.

"You just say, 'Good on you,' to the kid, but then you're thinking he tops out in the AHL," said the veteran NHL scout. "There are a few guys over the years right in that profile—pretty prolific scoring in the league at nineteen, but without the breakout skill or assets to play in the NHL. At his size, he needed to be a plus-plus skater [to make the NHL], and I didn't think he was there at all."

Brown was a feel-good story when he landed with the Marlies— a kid in the AHL who kept a backyard rink in Etobicoke, played his minor hockey with the Marlies, and still lived with his parents, even while the Leafs were signing his paycheck. As an atom, he had his photo taken in his Marlies sweater next to George Armstrong, who famously scored the Leafs' last Cup-clinching goal in 1967. Brown still looked like the kid in the picture, with his red hair, fair complexion, and conspicuous lack of razor stubble, more like a paperboy than a future NHLer. And on the 2015–16 Marlies, all the attention was on William Nylander, Kasperi Kapanen, and others. Brown was just the kid who was happy to be there. Supposedly, anyway.

When the Leafs made their call-ups at the end of the tank season, Brown fell in among them. Nylander stood out, but Brown wound up with a goal and six assists in seven games. Even after that performance, he wasn't expected to make the team in the fall. Others stood in front of him; the numbers were against him. The team had just signed free agent Seth Griffith, who had led the AHL in assists while playing in Boston's organization, and Josh Leivo had spent more time with the Marlies. The team had more reasons for sending Brown down. But come the start of the season, the Leafs had committed to Brown, Griffith would soon be gone, and Leivo was back down to the Marlies, effectively passed.

Maybe the handwriting had been on the wall for Griffith and Leivo. After all, Brown had been a favourite of Babcock from day one.

"He was our best kid in training camp," Babcock told the *Globe and Mail* back in the spring of 2016, when Brown was called up from the Marlies. "He has elite hockey sense, and he'll be an NHLer for a long time."

Throughout the 2016–17 season, Babcock would shuttle Brown onto a line with Matthews and Hyman when Nylander sputtered and made poor plays in the Toronto end. And Brown became a go-to player for Babcock on the penalty kill and landed second-unit power-play shifts. Alone among the Leafs' rookie forwards, he could fit into any game situation.

Not all of the Leafs rookies could have a backstory like Matthews's. Some of them were comparable—Nylander's history overlapped with Kapanen's; Brown was a product of the GTHL, as was Marner. But the rookie whose story Brown's most resembled was another product of Toronto's minor hockey system: Zach Hyman. So, it was predictable that the two would become good friends and training partners during the summer. Like Brown, Hyman made the NHL more on hockey sense and will than natural gifts or developed skills. Hyman didn't play for his father, but his father, Stuart Hyman, was an influential figure in the GTHL, arguably the most influential—at one point in the early 2000s, Stuart, a Toronto real estate developer, owned ninety GTHL organizations. Owning a kids' hockey team might seem like a hobby or community service, but the fact is that many teams were worth six figures, some as much as an estimated $300,000. (Hyman stepped away from minor hockey in the city in 2004.)

Ukraine-born coach Boris Dorozhenko (left) played a key role in Matthews's development in Phoenix, putting him through innovative workouts that professionals sometimes failed to finish. *Boris Dorozhenko*

Lou Lamoriello (left of Auston Matthews) never had a first overall pick in his years in New Jeresy, nor did Mike Babcock (far right) in Detroit and Anaheim. *Getty Images/Bruce Bennett*

To manage the Leafs, team president Brendan Shanahan recruited his first GM in the pros, Lou Lamoriello, and the coach in his final year in Detroit, Mike Babcock. *Canadian Press*

Mike Babcock's eight-year $50-million contract was the largest ever tendered an NHL coach. *Getty Images/Kevin Sousa*

Matthews, here scoring his fourth goal against Ottawa, made an unprecedented NHL debut. Only three players in the last 70 years had recorded a hat trick in their first NHL games. *Getty Images/Icon Sportswire*

Matthews celebrating a goal against the Oilers in November. Matthews endured a couple of prolonged slumps yet shattered the Leafs' rookie scoring record with 40 regular-season goals. *Getty Images/Codie McLachlan*

Mitch Marner, taking a selfie with a snake around his neck on the NHL draft-prospects tour, would later catch heat for a photo with a fish. Connor McDavid looks on from the left. *Getty Images/Eliot J. Schechter*

Many doubted whether Marner, here throwing a puck to a kid celebrating his birthday, would even be big enough at age nineteen to withstand play in the NHL. *Getty Images/Kevin Sousa*

Wendel Clark visits Marner and Matthews prior to the Centennial Classic. Clark was the last Maple Leafs rookie to generate the sort of buzz like that of the class of 2016–17. *Getty Images/Graig Abel*

Toronto fans had long despaired other cities' landing the NHL's New Year's outdoor games, but the 2017 Centennial Classic was a spectacle and historic occasion worth waiting for. *Getty Images/Icon Sportswire*

Brendan Shanahan was named one of the NHL's 100 greatest players in the league's centennial year during a ceremony before the All-Star Game in Los Angeles. Here he accepts congratulations from Auston Matthews, who made the game at age nineteen. *Getty Images/Andrew D. Bernstein*

Fans had worried that the Leafs' rookies would lose games to injuries, as many first-year players do. Except for a few games Marner lost to a shoulder injury, they managed to stay on the ice all season. The scariest injury might have been in a game against Buffalo, when Rielly collided with Sabres forward William Carrier, above, and fell awkwardly into the boards. *Getty Images/Graig Abel*

Zach Hyman, here on the ice after a hard hit, played the most physical game of the Leafs rookies but, at age twenty-four, he was the one most ready for the NHL grind. *Getty Images/Kevin Sousa*

Jake Gardiner had been a rookie on the Leafs team that suffered a heart-breaking Game 7 overtime loss in Boston in 2013. Here he celebrates a goal with Mitch Marner in happier times. *Getty Images/Mark Blinch*

Mitch Marner and Connor Brown butt helmets in a pregame routine. Both won Ontario Hockey League scoring titles, though few saw the latter even sticking in the OHL. *Getty Images/Kevin Sousa*

Kasperi Kapanen's first NHL goal came late in Game 81 against Pittsburgh, when the Leafs' playoff hopes were dangling by a thread. *Getty Images/Graig Abel*

Trade-deadline addition Brian Boyle gives advice to Hyman in a playoff game against Washington. Boyle would artfully set up Kapanen's overtime winner in Game 2 against the Capitals. *Getty Images/Mark Blinch*

While hockey fans have made jokes about a Toronto Stanley Cup parade for years, there's no scene in the NHL like the crowd that gathers out on Maple Leafs Square during games home and away. *Getty Images/ Icon Sportswire*

Tyler Bozak is mobbed by teammates after scoring in overtime in Game 3, giving the Leafs a series advantage against Washington. *Getty Images/Mark Blinch*

The Leafs salute fans at the Air Canada Centre after losing Game 6 in overtime to the Capitals and being eliminated from the playoffs. *Getty Images/Mark Blinch*

"You see a lot of parents investing in their kids' future, whether they have a future in the game or not," said one NHL scout who had tracked minor hockey in Toronto. "That usually amounts to personal coaching, hockey schools, equipment, or whatever. Zach Hyman's father took it to an extreme."

The extreme included the purchase of International Scouting Services (ISS), an outfit that compiles ratings of NHL prospects, an independent version of NHL Central Scouting, the league's in-house evaluators of draft-eligible players. ISS ranked Zach Hyman 120th in his draft year when he was playing for the Hamilton Red Wings, a Junior A team owned by his father. By contrast, Central Scouting had him in the 200s. Hyman wound up being selected by Florida 123rd overall in the 2010 NHL entry draft. In the end, the ranking by the outfit owned by his father had a far more accurate read on him than did that of Central Scouting—and even with that, ISS seemed to have underrated him.

The career paths of Hyman and Brown first overlapped in Junior A the season after Hyman's draft year, one year before Brown's. While Brown was a not-quite point-a-game sixteen-year-old with St. Mike's, Hyman put up more than 100 points in forty-three games with Hamilton.

College had been a fallback option for Brown, but it was the direction Hyman was always headed in. He had been an honours student at a Hebrew high school in Toronto, and always had an intellectual curiosity. A short story he wrote for an assignment as a twelve-year-old would not only win a prize in a major children's writing contest but years later be published as a children's book—*Hockey Hero*—and earn him a multi-book deal with a major publisher.

"Writing is something that I'm always going to do," he said. "That's what my plan is after hockey, but I'll be writing and thinking about writing while I'm in the game. I was always really interested in storytelling traditions—I remember sitting and listening to my grandfather and family telling their stories, and that's what I want to do: tell stories that inspire young people."

Hyman's performance that season as an eighteen-year-old with the Hamilton Junior A club helped land him a full ride to the University of Michigan, one of the most desired destinations in the NCAA ranks. In Hyman's freshman and sophomore years at Michigan, it seemed like he had a much brighter future in literature than in hockey—he had but nine points in each season and was far from in favour with the coach, Red Berenson. By his senior year, though, Hyman had turned it around. With 24 goals and 54 points in thirty-seven games, Hyman was a finalist for the Hobey Baker Award, the NCAA's highest honour. Hyman was also a finalist for the Coach Wooden Citizenship Award—the award recognizing collegiate athletes for "excellence both on and off the field [and as] role models both as performers and persons." The coach who had reluctantly doled out ice time to Hyman as a freshman became his most strident advocate.

"Some kids just expect things to be handed to them because that's how they've been brought up," Berenson told the *Globe and Mail*. "[Hyman's] from a privileged background, but he doesn't act like that. He's going to play a blue-collar game, even though when he walks into the rink, he may not look like a blue-collar person."

Because Hyman had played out his entire four-year college eligibility, the rights that the Panthers had acquired in the draft were due to lapse in the summer of 2015—Hyman would become a free agent. Florida made its pitch, but Hyman wasn't interested, and the Panthers traded his rights to the Maple Leafs. He quickly signed with them.

"They're going to get a kid that bleeds blue and white, understands the tradition of the Maple Leafs, and who has always dreamed of being a Maple Leaf," Stuart Hyman told the *Star*. "He'll be proud to wear that uniform."

The plot of *Hockey Hero* follows a shy kid who makes the NHL. While Hyman's own story is much more complicated than that—with his father's ownership of teams, free agency, and the like—from Hyman's vantage point, it may have seemed that he was just following the story he'd written. How it would end, though, was yet to be determined.

CHAPTER TEN

ALL SEASON, LEAFS MANAGEMENT HAD TRIED TO PROTECT THE players from the media. The message: Make one misstep and you'll open yourself up to criticism, so stick to the talking points, and remember that if something can be taken the wrong way, it inevitably will be. The perfect streak of every-word-measured had stretched through March. Then it went ever so slightly sideways one innocent day on a road trip. If any of the Leafs, young or old, thought that the approach had been taken to a ridiculous extreme, they came away with an object lesson in the risks of going off message, enough to scare the boys back into the bubble. To whatever extent it had dawned on them that they were celebrities, they came around to appreciate the price that goes with it.

The Leafs' schedule in mid-March called for a three-game swing through the Southeast Division: Carolina Saturday night, the Panthers in Fort Lauderdale on Tuesday, and Tampa Bay on Thursday. The team flew out to Fort Lauderdale after the game in Raleigh, a nondescript win, but a win nonetheless. It looked like there was only upside ahead, too: a two-day layover in Fort Lauderdale before game day. It also turned out that the Leafs' visit to the Atlantic side coincided with March break. At the Leafs' hotel, you could see some adults by the pool, while the beach was crowded with rowdy college-aged kids exercising their right to behave badly. It was, at some level, an alien experience to the players. While other kids that they'd grown up with would have headed to Florida in their late teens for spring break, there had been no such luck for the players, who spent their time off from school playing hockey. Last March, Matthews had been in Switzerland; Marner in London, Ontario; Nylander on the bus with the Marlies. A lot of the frat boys down for spring break were the age of Morgan Rielly, ostensibly a veteran on the Leafs. The kids in their teens and early twenties on the beach were decompressing and letting loose—what happens on spring break, stays on spring break—but every year, hockey players, no matter at what level of the game, are gearing up for the most important games of their season in the push to the playoffs.

With the compression of the schedule, it's a small blessing when a team gets two days off between games. It's also a small feat of juggling for teams to squeeze in off-days as mandated by the agreement with the NHLPA—four days a month with no practice or workouts, no access for media, and no meetings. Pure leisure. Sunday was designated as that day of rest. That the Leafs were also giving the players rooms at a five-star place looking out over the ocean and handing out meal money was doing the players a kindness.

For NHL teams on a swing through Florida, the standard off-day R&R is golf. Teams often book rounds ahead for an intramural event. The Leafs, however, broke into smaller groups for other diversions. Mitch Marner went fishing with his centre, Tyler Bozak, along with Leo Komarov, Morgan Rielly, and Josh Leivo. Social media erupted when Marner and Komarov posted selfies of the five of them together, shirtless, with one of their catches.

That was two days before game day. The team was on the ice the next morning, and Babcock liked the pace of the practice. His team seemed refreshed, buoyant. That night they saw their rivals for the last playoff spot in the conference, the Islanders, get pummeled 8–4 by the Hurricanes. The Panthers were banged up, missing a lot of their frontline players, and out of the playoff mix. And the Leafs would be facing James Reimer, their former teammate, who had been struggling mightily, losing his last seven starts. The Leafs had knocked the Panthers off back in midwinter when they had rolled through a Florida swing. Never are two points a given, but everything was trending towards a Toronto win and a climb back into a playoff spot.

Twenty-four hours later, though, the Leafs were coming off their worst game of the calendar year: a 7–2 loss to the Panthers.

However you cut the numbers, it could hardly have looked worse. Frederik Andersen gave up three goals on nine shots in the first period and sat the rest of the night. Nazem Kadri was minus-5. Bozak and Komarov were minus-4. Throw a dart at the Toronto side of the score sheet and it would hit an ugly number. The ugliest numbers were those in the Eastern Conference standings. With the loss and other action around the league, the Leafs were sitting in tenth place, outside the playoffs looking in.

It wasn't an easy loss to shrug off, but no one took the loss harder than Nikita Zaitsev. On a night when many had bad moments, he'd had the worst of all on the goal that gave Florida a 2–0 lead. The Leafs were on a power play and pressing when the puck came back to Zaitsev at the point. What happened next defies easy explanation. Untouched and facing no pressure, Zaitsev took an awkward spill—you'd have presumed he caught an edge, then lost another and skated over a man-of-war. Colton Sceviour took the puck and set off on a 150-foot breakaway, and Zaitsev gave vain chase—though it might not have been in vain had it not been for Bozak accidentally tripping his teammate. Sceviour deked out Andersen, and the game was two-zip in the most awful way.

Bozak afterward didn't equivocate. "A lot of it was mistakes, mistakes that aren't characteristic," the centre said.

Babcock did his best to keep a cool head, but managed only in part. "You think you should be good. You think you should be rested. You think you should be jumping," he said. "The bottom line is whatever we did, we didn't handle it right. We had one day off and practice, so that's not the end of the world. Whatever we did, we didn't get prepared."

The coach put the team on notice. Any idea that the Leafs might have a light skate on Wednesday was out. "There's a fine line between keeping the motor running and being away from the rink," said Babcock. "The other thing that has to happen, if you don't play good, you go to the rink. Period. It's that simple. The ball is in their court. No one minds a little downtime as long as you're ready to play when the puck is dropped at night."

The next morning, the Leafs were greeted by a gale-force tweetstorm, less critical of their performance Tuesday night than their fishing trip on Sunday. *For those of you players new to the city, welcome to Toronto.* Thankfully, they were out of earshot of the phone-in callers who said that the players should have been working on their breakout drills rather than their tans. The object lesson for the young Leafs: You don't have to do anything wrong to garner bad press if the optics are bad and you lose.

At the practice in Tampa the next day, you had to feel for Zaitsev. When asked if it helped to have a short memory after being routed 7–2 by Florida in Fort Lauderdale Tuesday night, Zaitsev sat at his stall and didn't raise his head. "I don't have a short memory," he said. "Maybe that's my problem."

Coach Mike Babcock had shuffled his blueline as the game got away from his team—Zaitsev had been playing beside Morgan Rielly on the number one pairing for most of the season, but as the night darkened and the Panthers pulled away, he was switched to partner with Jake Gardiner. All in all, it was the type of night that veterans can move past more easily than rookies.

If you had a short memory, you'd have forgotten where the season started, with Zaitsev an utterly unknown commodity, a never-drafted free agent signed out of the KHL at age twenty-four. Sure, he had lined up for the Russians in the World Cup, but then again, the country had been pretty thin for star candidates to carry the flag on the back end.

If you had a short memory, you'd have forgotten how Zaitsev landed on Rielly's side in training camp and started the season by matching up against opponents' top lines. He fared better than you could reasonably expect of a player who was seeing the league for the first time. That Zaitsev had hung in there so long before things went sideways was one of the lesser miracles in a Toronto Maple Leafs season that hadn't lacked for surprises.

A lot of players had been given the opportunities of their young lifetimes—at some point in the not-so-distant future, Zach Hyman will tell his kids about the days he played beside Auston Matthews. *Good times.* You wouldn't have said that of Zaitsev, though. He had been put in a position to fail and had persevered. It made sense—he had more skin in the game than the rest of the Leafs' rookies.

Zaitsev was a member of a Russian team that won one of the most memorable world junior titles in the tournament's history. Back in 2011, Zaitsev was a top-four blueliner for a team that, down 3–0 to Canada in the third period of the final in Buffalo, stormed back with five unanswered goals to claim a gold medal. A gold medal, however, was not a guaranteed ticket to the pros for the young Russians. Only five of the Russian teens then playing in the KHL had been drafted by NHL teams, most notably Vladimir Tarasenko and Evgeni Kuznetsov, selected by St. Louis and Washington, respectively. On its face, it seemed ridiculous—the Canadian team the Russians had beaten, a Canadian team playing in front of an arena full of raucous fans in Hockey Canada sweaters, had fourteen first-round draft picks in the line-up. All the other Canadian players in the game had been selected by NHL clubs in later rounds. Every player the Canadian coaches had cut in the tryouts was property of an NHL club. But, like most of his teammates, Zaitsev seemingly had no prospects of playing in the NHL in the near future—and things barely seemed brighter down the line.

"Nikita was one of those lost-generation Russian players," said Daniel Milstein, Zaitsev's Ukraine-born, Ann Arbor–based agent. "He was caught in between in the politics of the game. As a young player, he got into a bad situation, like so many kids who played in that game in Buffalo . . . contracts with their KHL clubs that they couldn't get out of."

The issue for Zaitsev and so many of his teammates was, as Milstein suggested, contractual. NHL teams that drafted Russian players had a limited window to sign them to contracts or else they lost all rights to them. Thus NHL teams that drafted Russian players had to negotiate not only with the players and their agents but also with the KHL teams to whom the draftees were under contract. That is, they had to negotiate buyouts of existing KHL contracts. And back in 2011, few KHL teams were motivated sellers. Tarasenko and Kuznetsov were too good to let pass, top-five talents, and yet they dropped in the draft to sixteenth and twenty-second overall, passed over because NHL general managers feared getting stiff-armed by KHL clubs. GMs bailed out—if Canadian or American or Scandinavian kids were almost as good as a Russian on the scouts' list, they were going to get the nod simply because signing them was relatively headache-free.

Despite the economic hurdles, Zaitsev, like virtually all the players in the Russian junior line-up, still wanted to play in the NHL.

"It was something that players want to do," Zaitsev says. "We know of the league, of Ovechkin and Datsyuk and the others when we are young. Of course we want to play in the same league . . . on the same teams as them."

Zaitsev's chances of making good on his ambitions were hurt by the fact that, at age seventeen, the Moscow native had been selected fourth overall in the KHL draft by HC Sibir Novosibirsk, a team with no great record of negotiating with NHL teams. If Zaitsev had been able to stay with one of the Moscow clubs—CKSA, Dynamo, Spartak, or Atlant—it would have facilitated negotiations, given their record of working with NHL clubs. Or not, at least, in the short term, as Milstein pointed out.

"In the seasons before [the 2014 Olympics in] Sochi, the Russian hockey federation wanted to keep its best players in the KHL—if not Ovechkin and others, then its best young players. Everything was with an eye toward the Olympics. Zaitsev was a national-team-quality player. Novosibirsk wanted control over the player. The KHL wanted control over development. The federation just wanted to control. And, really, NHL money didn't have an impact, not with a lot of clubs. They were being underwritten by the Russian government—again, part of the Olympics initiative. So Nikita and a lot of players were caught up in it."

As the team had with Tarasenko, Novosibirsk traded Zaitsev to a club more willing to do business with the NHL—Moscow CKSA, formerly known as Red Army. Zaitsev had been an emerging talent with Novosibirsk, and he'd been on CKSA's radar since he had trained with the team as a teenager. After he played in a few games with the Russian squad at the 2013 world championships, CKSA made its push and leveraged enough political clout to get the player that its well-connected management wanted.

"CKSA had the kid over a barrel in a way," said one NHL executive not affiliated with the Maple Leafs. "They were going to deal for him [with Novosibirsk] if he'd sign a deal with the club over term, locking him up for three seasons, effectively to age twenty-five. If he didn't like it, well, he was going to be stuck with his original club for a while, and as far as the NHL goes, out of sight, out of mind."

If it seemed like Zaitsev had nothing but bad luck, it wasn't quite true. His biggest break came in the wake of the Olympics in Sochi. The KHL's financial model wasn't sustainable, at least without Vladimir Putin and the franchise-owning oligarchs propping it up. Even billionaires get tired of pouring in tens of millions, especially after their political motivation evaporated—they had hoped a gold medal in Sochi would give them great propaganda value, but they instead wound up with an Olympic team that crashed without a medal. It was time for cutting losses. As Milstein said, "Players could see a light, a way out."

The first who made it out and made good was left-winger Artemi Panarin, who, after turning twenty-four, signed a two-year contract as an undrafted free agent with Chicago before the 2015–16 season. The Maple Leafs had chased Panarin hard, but the Blackhawks prevailed—his base salary in Chicago in his rookie season was very modest, just over $800,000, but Panarin hit the jackpot with triple that in bonus money on his way to winning the Calder Trophy as the league's top rookie.

Zaitsev wanted to follow Panarin's lead and started sounding out NHL teams in the summer of 2015. The Leafs flew Zaitsev in for meetings and tests. They might have considered negotiating a buyout with Novosibirsk so that Zaitsev could suit up with the Leafs that fall, an arrangement that would have financially benefited the club far more than it would Zaitsev. GMs of other clubs stepped up, too, but Zaitsev was willing to wait.

CKSA was prepared to offer Zaitsev an extension of his contract, but he decided against the security of a long-term deal. It was a calculated risk—if he could get to the free market, if he could play out the term of his contract with CKSA, then he could take his talents to the highest bidder in the NHL. It would shorten his window, as it were, as he'd lose a couple of seasons of prime earning years in the NHL. Doing that, however, would still give him more leverage than if he had been drafted out of junior. And in his last season with CKSA, Zaitsev raised his game, earning a place on the KHL's First All-Star Team.

The gamble seemed to pay off. After that season, more than a dozen NHL teams called Milstein to explore signing Zaitsev as a free agent, some offering good terms with their deals, albeit at relatively modest salaries. Zaitsev and Milstein doubled down. Just as the defenceman had done in his final season with CKSA, he could set a much higher market value for himself if he could establish that he could play a significant role on an NHL team for a season, if he did enough to convince general managers that he could fill a role in the first or second blueline pair for a playoff team.

So, Zaitsev opted to sign with the Leafs on a one-year deal that would make him a free agent once more in the summer of 2017. He was betting on the team giving him a chance to play significant minutes, and his plan seemed to be working out—as the Leafs headed into their spring break, Zaitsev was leading all NHL rookies in minutes played. But Zaitsev was also betting on playing better than he did against the Panthers. He had to if he was to see through his long-term plan. A free fall in Mike Babcock's opinion, a demotion to the third pairing, an injury—any one of them could poison the waters, costing him years of play and millions of dollars in earnings. Minus-4 would have been hard to take for any player, but it was likely hardest of all for a player in a contract season. At least that's how it looked from Zaitsev's perspective, sitting in the dressing room after the loss to the Panthers. He knew that Lamoriello and the Leafs were in talks with his agent about a contract extension.

At practice the next day in Tampa, Zaitsev was shifted from Morgan Rielly's right side on the top pair and found himself next to Jake Gardiner, whose penchant for bad pinches and overly aggressive play was bound to make life a little more difficult for the rookie. It also meant that Zaitsev would see less ice time. Babcock had a rationale—Zaitsev had spent the season playing against opponents' top lines, and with Gardiner he would face less stressful assignments. With the loss to Florida and wins by everyone else chasing the number three spot in the Atlantic and the Eastern Conference's last wild-card spot, the Leafs' chances of making the postseason had fallen to below 40 percent, according to websites that calculate the odds.

Filing off the ice after practice at the Lightning's home arena, Zaitsev looked as grim as ever. His issue wasn't the fact that he was dwelling on the tough game the night before. It was that he failed to remember his breakout performances early in the season or Babcock's enthusiasm for his play—it was just four weeks earlier that the coach had called him "a better defender than we could have hoped for . . . ultra-competitive . . . smart" and said that "he wants to be great."

No one in the Leafs' dressing room was more motivated than Zaitsev to be great, and no one felt the same sort of urgency and pressure that Zaitsev did. It had already been a dizzying season for the first-year players. But Zaitsev wasn't just playing the game and practicing and walking through video with the coaches—no, Zaitsev was waiting for calls and texts from Milstein. Hockey was a game, sure, but for Zaitsev, at least, it was one he couldn't afford to lose.

For the Maple Leafs, it was going to be a constant escalation of stakes down the stretch—raising one game, then doubling down the next. The back end of the swing through the Sunshine State marked, as the cliché would have it, the biggest game of the season—not the first time in the season the phrase had been uttered, and far from the last. The biggest until the next. Toronto was just one of three teams chasing the most readily available playoff slot, the second wild card in the Eastern Conference. The Leafs were a point behind the Islanders and the Lightning. A loss to Tampa wouldn't have snuffed the Leafs' hopes, but, according to the online services that calculate the odds, their chances of making the playoffs would have dipped close to 30 percent for the first time since the fall.

The calculus used to glean those odds wouldn't have factored in something so unscientific as experience, something that no one in hockey would undervalue. The Leafs were chasing a pair of teams with playoff experience. The Islanders had made it into the second round the previous spring, where they lost to the Lightning. In turn, Tampa Bay then took Pittsburgh to seven games in the conference final—the Lightning fell short, but they gave the Penguins the stiffest challenge on the latter's way to becoming Stanley Cup champions again.

Going into this season, much more had been expected of the Islanders—and, especially, the Lightning—than the Leafs. The Lightning had been many people's pick to win the Cup—according to Vegas odds at one major sports book at the beginning of the season, the Bolts were second only to Chicago to win it all. Things had changed since then, but Tampa was still a well-established club. Yes, they were without Steven Stamkos, but then again, they had made it all the way to Game 7 against Pittsburgh a year earlier without their franchise player. And yes, they had been sellers at the deadline—GM Steve Yzerman had taken a look at the standings and hadn't liked his team's chances, so in February he let go of expiring contracts, moving their former Vezina finalist Ben Bishop to Los Angeles and their massive checking line centre, Brian Boyle, to the Leafs. Tampa Bay had six wins and an overtime loss to show for the eight games since the deadline, the single loss coming to the Penguins in Pittsburgh. If Yzerman had thrown in the towel on the team's season, his team had thrown it back at him.

The Leafs' recent form was trending in the opposite direction—at best they were treading water. Toronto's leadership wasn't fooled by the three unimpressive wins over teams destined to miss the playoffs the week before—with the embarrassing loss in Fort Lauderdale, Toronto had just 9 points in its last nine games. Matthews hadn't had a point in the calendar month, and his shots on goal were falling off. You couldn't pick up any hint of fatigue in a given shift, but maybe Mike Babcock had: He had dialed down Matthews's ice time a minute or two a game, and in Tampa, the coach did the same once again, sending Matthews out for less than sixteen minutes for the first time in nineteen games. Fans might have been wondering what was wrong with Auston Matthews, even though he had a team-leading 31 goals.

All in all, the Leafs looked like a fragile team, and their run in late December seemed like a chimera. This appeared to be where it all would come undone—going south in the South. But then came one of the stranger turns of Toronto's already strange season.

It was a far from beautiful game. If you aren't in love with the NHL's contemporary brand of hockey and wanted to build a case for change, this would have been the game that you submitted into evidence. The watchword was caution, which is never a great descriptor when you're in an entertainment business. The game was played between the bluelines—the Lightning's defence was big and mobile enough to head off Toronto's young forwards on the rush and handle any attempts to play dump-and-chase. If the game was going to open up, it was going to take a goal, but it was hard to see one in the flow for either team—not that there was much flow at all.

Roman Polak finally broke the game open by scoring the game's first goal nine minutes into the first period. Tyler Bozak, the team's most adept centre on the draw, won an offensive-zone faceoff and put the puck cleanly onto Polak's waiting stick. Polak's shot from the point bounced off Tampa Bay starter Andrei Vasilevskiy high over his head—if it had been a baseball game, the infield fly rule would have applied. The puck flipped through the air and fell behind the goalie, trickling into the net as James van Riemsdyk waved at it, urging it across the line.

Polak's goal told the story of the game—it came on the Leafs' fourth shot of the game, and over the next eleven minutes, they managed just one more shot. It's not as though they were under a lot of heat, either—the home team managed only seven shots in the first period.

The most painful sequence for Tampa Bay came in the second period when Nikita Kucherov, the league's hottest shooter after the trading deadline, tried to deke Andersen at the edge of the crease and wound up throwing the puck into the corner of the rink, yards wide of the open net. It was that kind of night for the Lightning, and it only got worse.

In the second period, everything Toronto threw at the net seemed to go in. Rielly made it 2–0 a couple of minutes in, and Matt Martin beat Vasilevskiy just ten seconds later. With later goals by Connor Brown and van Riemsdyk, the Leafs held a 5–0 lead through the first thirty-five minutes and gave up only 14 shots in the process. By that point, the home team had stopped pushing back at all.

When the final buzzer sounded, it was good news all around for the Leafs. Their 5–0 win over the Lightning, combined with the Islanders' loss to Winnipeg, moved Toronto up from tenth in the conference to eighth.

After the game, Bozak stuck around to talk to reporters and

couldn't resist taking a shot at the fallout from the fishing trip. "Whenever you have a couple of days to bond as a group and do some stuff outside the rink, it really helps the team," he said, fighting to keep a straight face but eventually giving up. "I think it really helped us a lot tonight. We had a ton of energy and we played really well in a really good bounce-back game. It was a fun one to be a part of. With the magnitude of the game, for us to be able to do that is great."

Other than Brown's goal, the young Leafs didn't play large roles in the game—once again, Matthews didn't pick up a point, even after Babcock replaced Brown with Nylander on Matthews's right wing to try to get him going. That the Leafs were still in the hunt was, this night at least, thanks to the team's veteran corps.

"It's an incredibly delicate balance that you have to strike if you're bringing in a young player or two," said one NHL executive. "There has to be the right environment around them, the right team culture, to give them a chance to succeed, and a lot of good kids can struggle when they're just not around the right players and given the sort of support they need when they're just learning the league. They need to be walking into a good room every day. It's pretty clear that they have a good group in Toronto, and it's a credit to the veteran players. If there were ever any bad actors there, they sorted that out."

The NHL exec pointed to Buffalo as a team that wasn't doing its young players any favours, most notably Jack Eichel, Matthews's former teammate in Ann Arbor. In his second year in the league, Eichel was clearly frustrated with a Sabres team that was out of the playoff chase by Christmas and not convincingly concealing his disenchantment with coach Dan Bylsma. It's not a good look, having your twenty-year-old franchise centre standing in front of the media, doing damage control. Eichel wasn't alone in testing management's patience—Sam Reinhart, the second overall pick from the 2014 draft, was going to be benched for what Bylsma described as "a violation of team policy." The team didn't go into specifics, but the NHL exec who commended the Leafs said that the Sabres were "letting the young players get away from them . . . a leadership vacuum."

That was what was lost in the fallout from the fishing photos on Instagram. The Leafs had stumbled on the ice, and it had been easy to blame the failings on the team's youth. But what was missing in the furore was an acknowledgment of the Leafs' experience. The team's veterans—players like Bozak, Komarov, and Rielly—knew how to manage their jobs and guide the younger Leafs, who were figuring it all out during their first trip through the league. That experience might not have been as well developed as on other clubs, but this wasn't a team on which the young stars had no restraints and no one to answer to. True, they might sometimes need a reminder or rely on the veterans to catch them when they fell—but with only thirteen games remaining in the season, there were only so many more times the young Leafs could afford to make those mistakes.

CHAPTER ELEVEN

MIKE BABCOCK WOULD CLAIM THAT, BACK IN THE FALL, HE HAD told his team that if they were going to make the playoffs—with a big emphasis on *if*—it was going to come down to Game 82. And if it got to that point—with an equally big emphasis on *if*—then it was going to be a "crawl" into the last available playoff spot on the Eastern Conference grid. He was reinforcing what veteran players know, what certainly the handful of players who had been around for Game 7 in Boston knew: At least a couple of imperfect teams make it into the Stanley Cup playoffs. Sometimes very imperfect. Sixteen teams make it into the postseason, but at least a couple leave you scratching your head. It might have seemed hopelessly optimistic to give that why-not-us message to a team that finished last overall the season before.

As it turned out, it hadn't come down to Game 82. It had come down to Game 80, a win-and-you're-in tilt at the ACC against Toronto's nearest pursuer, Tampa Bay, a team that the Leafs had rolled over 5–0 in Florida just a few weeks before. The Lightning had been absolutely gutted by injury all season long. "If we had [Tampa's] injuries, we wouldn't have a sniff at the playoffs," Babcock said. And yet, coming into Toronto for Game 80 without Steven Stamkos, the Lightning had gone 6-0-1 in their last seven games and were still within sight of the playoffs. With the harsh mathematics of elimination constantly stacked against them, Tampa Bay had been playing with Game 7 urgency for weeks.

A less-than-hopelessly optimistic Leafs fan had to have presumed that Tampa Bay's adrenaline would eventually ebb, and that the flat effort against Washington a couple of nights before was simply a by-product of fatigue in the second of back-to-back games. A return to recent form seemed a fair shot. Including the loss to the Capitals, the Leafs had gone 7-2 in their last nine games. All the websites calculating the Leafs' odds of making the playoffs had them in the mid-90s going into the Tampa Bay game. Talk about Toronto landing a second seed in the Atlantic Division and home-ice advantage in the opening-round series didn't seem far-fetched. Casting further forward, a prospective match-up with the seemingly staggering and beat-up Ottawa Senators seemed to give more than a glimmer of hope for the Leafs to advance to the second round.

Matthews had fully snapped out of his seven-game goalless drought, which had run through early March—he had 8 goals in the ten games running up to the potential playoff clincher against the Lightning, and his 31 even-strength goals led the league. But as good as Matthews had been, as flashy as Marner continued to be, it was in fact Nylander who had been the Leafs' best rookie in the home stretch, maybe even their best player through that time, with the possible exception of Andersen. The Leafs' line-shuffling up front had come to an end, and Nylander was thriving in his role on Matthews's right wing. The league noticed Nylander's 4 goals and 10 assists in fourteen games in March and named him the league's Rookie of the Month for the second time in the season.

Despite the upward trends in the Leafs' favour, the team came out with its flattest effort since its loss to the Panthers a couple of weeks earlier. Brayden Point, an undersized rookie who had been thrust into a lead role in Stamkos's absence, scored twice in Tampa Bay's 4–1 win. The visiting team had directed the play from Nikita

Kucherov's goal midway through the second period right through to the end of the game.

"We didn't play like we normally do," Mike Babcock said. "I thought we were slow; I don't know if we were tight, but we weren't in sync. They won all the battles and all the races, and we never established the game we normally play." The coach admitted that he thought his team came down with a bad case of nerves. "We can't let the energy and excitement of the moment get in the way of who we are," he said, though he had no suggestion for how to head this off going into the last weekend of the season.

Just as worrisome as the flatline effort over sixty minutes was a single moment late in the first period that set the tone for the game. Matthews was gathering speed in the neutral zone and hitting the blueline without the puck when defenceman Jake Dotchin lined him up. Dotchin had been the perpetrator who had taken out Kapanen in the AHL two months before. Dotchin had also been on the other end of a flagrantly illegal play just a couple of nights before: a spear from Boston's Brad Marchand. Some would skate away from an assault like that and aspire to play a fair and clean game, but Dotchin didn't draw on that as the lesson. He seemed to take it as instructive and representative of the raised stakes in a desperate run to the playoffs—something along the lines of do-unto-others-before-they-can-do-unto-you. Dotchin stuck his right knee out into Matthews's path, and the Leafs rookie's left knee buckled. It could have been any player, but it wasn't. Things happen fast on the ice, but even in that split second, Dotchin must have known it was Matthews who was coming at him. And any chance to line up Matthews had the potential to affect not only the outcome of the game but also the games down the line—the help that Tampa Bay was going to need to get into the playoffs. There came a collective gasp from the crowd as

Matthews lay facedown on the ice, and then boos rained down when the referees didn't call a penalty.

Brian and Ema Matthews were in attendance. Though they hadn't seen the knee-on-knee hit that had cost their son the first half of his under-17 season in Ann Arbor, they knew from his retelling that it had looked an awful lot like Dotchin's. While Brian looked on impassively, Ema sat up in her seat and extended her hands, as if miming *You're kidding me.*

There had been hearts-in-the-mouth moments earlier in the season. Frederik Andersen had a reputation for fragility, but outside of the shot in the jaw that knocked him out of a game in Buffalo in late March, he had mostly held up. There had been worries about Marner's ability to stand up to contact in the men's league, but he had managed to stay out of harm's way, with the exception of the hit Columbus's Boone Jenner laid on him in February. (In a conversation after the season, Paul Marner suggested that his son had in fact played through what he described as a mild bout of mononucleosis, which made his continued presence in the line-up even more impressive.) And Tyler Bozak had been playing through a wrist injury that had kept him out of practice throughout the late winter and early spring. The Leafs' 133 man-games-lost put the team sixth best in the league, not what you'd expect of a team with so many young players in the line-up, so many going through the NHL grind for the first time. It would be tempting to put it down to dumb luck, though luck certainly had something to do with it. Behind the scenes, though, the Leafs' medical staff had availed themselves of all that sports science had to offer to track the players' health and well-being. In previous managements, health maintenance had been the subject of some second-guessing. The Leafs' new style of play had to factor into it. It wasn't a heavy game they played. It wasn't a percussive one. The new Leafs gained the puck by diligence and speed rather than by knocking players along the wall into next week. Even on the blueline, outside of Polak, the big hits were few. Matthews skated into heavy traffic and went into the dirty areas boldly, but the likes of Nylander and Marner picked their spots and relied on stealth.

Thankfully, Matthews made it back into the Tampa game, not missing a shift. Watching him closely, though, you wondered if he was feeling the effects. He didn't seem his usual self as the game got away from the Leafs.

The next day, Matthews noted that come the end of the season, everyone was playing with "something or another." In the NHL, the wounded—at least those whose wounds are disclosed at all—are designated to have either "an upper-body injury" or "a lower-body injury." If Matthews and the others were banged up, how much game would they have playing their fourth and fifth games in seven nights?

After the loss to Tampa Bay, the irrational enthusiasm of the week before evaporated. The Leafs were entering the final weekend of the season needing two points from two games. Both games were at home, which was promising. Both, less promisingly, were against league heavyweights: defending Stanley Cup champions Pittsburgh, and then Columbus, the team with the third best record in the Eastern Conference. If the Leafs' historical run of bad luck held out, Babcock's preseason prediction could be turned inside out with a couple of too easily imagined losses. The awful prospect loomed: that this young team might only fall out of playoff contention in Game 82.

The Penguins waddled in with nothing to play for in the last weekend of the season, having already tucked home ice in the first round of the playoffs into their tiny little pockets. They didn't have their best defencemen, Kris Letang and Olli Maatta, who were out due to injury. They opted not to dress Evgeni Malkin, Chris Kunitz, and Carl Hagelin—they were all listed as day-to-day, and coach Mike Sullivan had decided that this game was not going to be that particular day. A team with nothing to play for and a bunch of scrubs in the line-up seemed like easy picking.

But Sidney Crosby has only a push-button booster, no cruise control, no on-off toggle switch. And say what you will about Phil, but he'll always be Kesseling. And while other players might not bring as much skill to the rink, anyone who steps onto the ice is capable of mayhem. All of these combined to give Leafs fans agita right from the opening puck-drop.

Kessel struck first, crossing up defenceman Morgan Rielly and wiring a shot past Frederik Andersen in the first period. The volume of the boos turned up when fans realized who had scored; they thought Kessel looked all too happy about it.

Early on, the Leafs' best player was a veteran, one whose name had been a fixture in mid-season trade rumours: James van Riemsdyk. JVR tied the game a half minute after Kessel's goal with a stunning bit of skill—in stride, deflecting a puck that was waist-high and behind him as he split defenders at the blueline, and then deking Marc-André Fleury. On his next two shifts, van Riemsdyk had two other glorious scoring chances turned aside by Fleury. The rout and the playoffs were seemingly on JVR's stick.

The scariest moment came with the game tied one-all a couple of minutes into the second period. Pittsburgh's Tom Sestito, a thuggish six-foot-five forward who had spent most of the season in the AHL, earned a two-minute minor and the enduring enmity of Leafs' fans when he clocked Andersen. Andersen was down on the ice, motionless, for a good minute, with a trainer hovering over him. Even when Andersen made it to his knees, it was clear he wasn't fit to continue. Curtis McElhinney was rushed back into service. On the ensuring power play, Nylander set up Tyler Bozak for the go-ahead goal, but a thin lead seemed like poor revenge and a poorer trade-off for the loss of the number one goalie.

It looked less attractive when, a few minutes later, Crosby did what Crosby does. His league-leading 44th goal of the season came on the power play and knotted the game. The awful sinking feeling that the Leafs' season might last only three more full periods crept into fans' stomachs. And it only got worse. Seven minutes into the third, Pittsburgh rookie Jake Guentzel took a shot that was going wide of the net until Jake Gardiner tried to kick it up onto his stick. Instead, he kicked the puck past McElhinney. Gardiner, much criticized for making routine plays perilous and for bad pinches at the worst times, bent over as a hush fell across the ACC. Pittsburgh had a 3–2 lead, and if the playoff bubble was going to burst, Gardiner's own-goal would be revisited over and over in the season's wake.

It looked dark, often very dark, for the Maple Leafs' run to a playoff berth, all the way up to the fifty-seventh minute, when Gardiner's self-esteem was salvaged by two rookies, albeit not the most likely ones.

Kaspari Kapanen had been brought up to the team only a couple of weeks before to fill in for the injured Nikita Soshnikov on the fourth line, not exactly what he might have had in mind when he was telling NHL teams that he saw himself as "a pure scorer," and not the role he had been groomed for with the Marlies. He often seemed miscast on the fourth line beside Boyle and Matt Martin, skating hard but accomplishing little—there was no learning curve for Kapanen, no time to break in. Rather than shorten his bench and lean on Matthews's and Bozak's lines, Babcock had thrown the fourth line out on the ice with less than six minutes to go, and, with the Leafs crowding Fleury, the puck came free to Kapanen. Fleury was sprawled on the ice with the net wide open—and Kapanen didn't miss. His goal produced a roar as new life pumped into the team's veins.

The Leafs weren't done there. Connor Brown had been buzzing Fleury's net all night long. With under three minutes left in regulation, he threw the puck back to Rielly on the right point, who fired a shot wide. The puck bounced around the Penguins' end before coming back to Gardiner at the opposite end of the blueline. Brown was being held up by Kevin Porter, a thirty-one-year-old pro journeyman in just his second game since being called up from the AHL. Just as Gardiner got a shot off, Brown freed himself from Porter's marking and got the blade of his stick on the puck, opening it enough on his forehand to deflect it high towards the top corner. Fleury might have heard the puck hit Brown's stick, but that was it—Kadri was standing directly in front of him, and the Pens goalie had no chance to react. The Leafs were back in the lead.

Brown seemed to channel the crowd's elation, leaping on the spot as Kadri skated out and wrapped his arms around him before the rest of the Leafs on the ice joined in. Fleury stood motionless, but gliding by the celebration was Kessel, who glanced at his four former teammates and the rookie before turning away. Brown took off and skated along the boards, accepting high fives from his teammates. The arena roared—on the TV broadcast the picture jiggled as if the arena had been struck by an earthquake. And when the game score went up on the Internet, it had to prompt double takes: Did Brown really have 20 goals on the season? That would have been enough to be the leading rookie goal scorer on twenty-seven other NHL teams.

Pittsburgh tried to mount a counterattack, but with Fleury pulled in favour of an extra skater in the last minute, McElhinney made a couple of superior saves on Crosby to preserve the one-goal advantage. In the dying seconds, Matthews shot the puck into the vacated net, his 40th goal of the season, one that, like his winner in the Centennial Classic, paid out a six-figure bonus.

The Leafs had made the playoffs.

Coach Mike Babcock had an interesting take on it: To his mind, big games make veterans better and young guys nervous. Maybe that was true for JVR and McElhinney, among others, but in the end, it was a couple of rookies—the less heralded ones at that—who made the difference in the Leafs' biggest game in the four years since that awful night in Boston.

For the first thirty minutes of Game 82 against Columbus, fans were putting it in their calendars: Games 1 and 2 against the Senators in Ottawa. The Leafs needed just one point in their final regular-season game the next night to reboot the Battle of Ontario.

But in a season with many points squandered in shoot-out losses, the Leafs were just one point short of their desired match-up. A loss to Columbus would leave Toronto as the second wild card in the Eastern Conference, with the daunting task of taking on Washington, where the Presidents' Trophy–winning Capitals awaited. It seemed even more intimidating after the loss to Columbus, because the Leafs looked like a team that had given everything to get to Game 82 and who now had nothing left in reserve.

Mike Babcock said that his team was drained by the last six weeks of the season and finally tapped by the come-from-behind victory over Pittsburgh.

"[The Pittsburgh game] was emotional," Babcock said. "I was worried whether we'd have enough juice. We had to go 14-5-1 to get [into the playoffs], and a lot of those games were tough."

On the face of it, Columbus might have seemed ready for the taking. Like Pittsburgh, the Blue Jackets came to the ACC with nothing at stake—they had locked up third place in the Metropolitan Division and were aiming to come out of Sunday night unbruised. They were already looking ahead to their own first-round match-up against their own bitter rivals, the defending Cup champion Penguins.

The outlook for the Leafs in Game 82 and any games down the line darkened when Babcock submitted the line-up: Frederik Andersen, the number one goalie, didn't dress. The Leafs provided no information about his status beyond the standard "upper-body injury," and no timeline was given for his return. For the last game of the regular season, though, Curtis McElhinney was far from the worst fallback. After all, he had come in for Andersen Saturday to get the W against Pittsburgh. And he was certainly not lacking personal motivation for the Columbus game: the Blue Jackets had waived him in midseason. Whatever the falloff might have been from Andersen to McElhinney was more than offset by the Blue Jackets' selection for the last assignment of the regular season: Columbus was giving their Vezina-worthy number one, Sergei Bobrovsky, the night off and going with backup Joonas Korpisalo. McElhinney had a .918 save percentage coming into the game, Korpisalo .902. It looked like advantage Toronto.

For the first ten minutes of Game 82, the Leafs were pitching the ultimate shutout. Dominating puck possession, the Leafs didn't allow the Blue Jackets to register a shot over that span. Columbus finally broke through and tested McElhinney a couple of times in the first period, but the shots stood 12–6 at the intermission, a promising sign for the home team. If anything, the Leafs looked energized by the win over Pittsburgh. It seemed as though they were heading into the postseason with confidence and momentum.

When James van Riemsdyk scored twice early in the middle frame, Leafs fans opened their travel apps, looking for hotel rooms in Ottawa. The superstitious would claim that what happened next is what happens when you tempt fate. As Babcock feared, the Leafs hit the bottom of their carton of juice, and not a drop was left.

McElhinney's work rate went from zero to harried. After not seeing a puck in the first ten minutes of the game, McElhinney faced 17 shots in a twenty-minute stretch. Fatigue played a part in this shift in the flow of the game, but so did the loss of two key defencemen, Nikita Zaitsev and Roman Polak. The pair, both right-handed shots, were knocked out of the game in the second period. The veteran Polak returned after treatment, but only for a shift. The Russian rookie was pounded into the glass on a hard but legal check by Blue Jackets captain Nick Foligno and struggled just to get back on his skates and off the ice; he was taken to the Leafs' dressing room for examination, per the league's concussion protocol. Up on press row, the Leafs announced that Zaitsev had suffered "a lower-body injury." A few minutes later, the team corrected this to "an upper-body injury" and stated that he was done for the game, exactly what everyone who had seen the hit had presumed on impact. The Leafs had to go with two-thirds of their already weary blueline corps and Morgan Rielly switching to his wrong side against the Columbus forwards, who were looking for a chance to fatten their stats.

"It makes it tough when you're down to four D in the second game of a back-to-back," van Riemsdyk said. Too tough in Game 82.

Over a seven-minute stretch to close out the second period, the Blue Jackets scored all the goals they'd need to dispatch the Leafs. Matt Calvert and Josh Anderson tied the game, and the pesky, undercelebrated all-star Cam Atkinson notched the third, his 35th goal of the season. On Anderson's goal in particular, the Leafs' fatigue was plain—Jake Gardiner tried to pivot to get back into the play and seemed to seize up.

The Leafs did manage to outshoot Columbus 11–6 in the third period, but only a couple of times did they look like a real threat to come away with a point. Auston Matthews had the best chance to tie the game and send the team off to Ottawa—with six minutes to go he crashed Korpisalo's goal and had the goaltender down, but the puck brushed off the post. In his last couple of strides going to the net, it looked like Matthews's knees buckled; even the young legs on the team were filled with sand.

The Leafs lost the game, and with it, their desired narrative. They weren't going to face Ottawa, a series many had believed winnable; instead, they faced the league's best team during the regular season, Washington. The status of the Leafs' number one goalie was unknown, the worst possible situation for any team bound for the playoffs. Compounding the misery was the fact that their top two right-handed defencemen had been knocked out of the Columbus game. Even if they were hale and hearty, the assignment of marking Alexander Ovechkin was a stiff challenge, and if they couldn't play, the Capitals' star figured to eat the fill-ins alive. Just twenty-four hours after the Saturday night game against Pittsburgh, the joy about Toronto's postseason chances had fully subsided. The Leafs weren't going into the playoffs on a high. They were going in with question marks. The team had stayed remarkably healthy all season, but, down to the last strokes, the status of three key players was suddenly uncertain—in fact, you could build a case that the three players they were losing were the toughest on the team to replace, so pronounced was the falloff to their substitutes. With the timing and the match-up, the outlook for an extended series wasn't promising. Given that the Leafs had gone 1-3 in the last four games of the season, all at home, it would have been hard to like their chances against any team in the postseason.

With Game 82 behind them, the Leafs might have deemed the end of the season an appropriate time to take stock. The Maple Leafs' year had been the furthest thing from the tank season that Dave Pal and the others at TKO's had resigned themselves to.

Back in September, there had been talk of working Matthews into the line-up gradually, of giving Marner a shot at playing some games with the big club and then sending him back to London for one last junior season, of Nylander maybe not being a great fit with Babcock's approach to coaching. Twenty staffers at nhl.com, as well as NHL Network on-air personalities, had made their predictions for the season: None had placed the Leafs in the playoffs. In the chat rooms and websites like Pension Plan Puppets, most Leafs partisans—maybe all of them—had given the Leafs a shot at making a run at the playoffs, but they'd figured the chase would fall just short.

Teams come out of seemingly nowhere to make a run for a season, and on that count the Leafs weren't alone in 2016–17—the Canadian Press actually had the Columbus Blue Jackets finishing second to last in the Eastern Conference. Seeing the Leafs' season unfold game by game almost inured you to how remarkable it truly was. It would have been one thing if a few veterans were able to summon their former glories for a single run, a nice send-off. This, however, was the exact opposite.

The regular season had ended as it had started, with Matthews in the forefront. He led the team in scoring with 40 goals and 69 points, a remarkable feat on several counts. For one, he had endured a couple of goalless and pointless slumps during the season, which his outbursts at other times had more than made up for. He did lead all Leafs forwards in ice time with an average of 17:38, but really that amounted to one more shift per game than Leo Komarov. Seeing numbers like the ones Matthews posted, you might have presumed that he was an automatic choice to roll over the boards with the first power-play unit. But that was far from the case. It had typically been Bozak or Kadri out there to win the face-offs in the offensive zone, with van Riemsdyk standing in front of the opponents' net and Marner working his magic along the wall. Kadri's 12 power-play goals led the team, and Nylander had 9, one more than Matthews. It was a tough unit to crack: with 58 goals and a 23.8 percent success rate, the Leafs' power play was the league's second-most efficient. There was nothing vaguely hollow about Matthews's goal totals—he led the league in even-strength goals with 31, one better than Carolina's Jeff Skinner and two ahead of Crosby. He got more done with less than anyone in the league—his time-on-ice ranked forty-seventh among league centres, eighty-seventh among all forwards.

Other aspects of Matthews's game remained a work in progress. His face-off percentage was below average for an NHL centre at 47 percent, but that still compared favourably with other franchise centres when they were teenagers—not as good as Jonathan Toews's 53 percent in his rookie season, but better than Crosby's 45.5.

Both Marner and Nylander weren't far behind Matthews in points, each scoring 61 apiece. Marner benefited from familiarity, playing the entire season beside Bozak. In contrast, Babcock shuffled Nylander through the line-up. If Babcock had been looking for a correction in Nylander's game, he'd found it. Nylander finished the season where he started it, on Matthews's right wing, and although he was the oldest of the three, he almost indisputably improved the most as the season played out.

As with everything else in the season, the success had started with the three rookies at the top, but it didn't end there. Brown's 20 goals were impressive at a glance, but even more so when you considered that, at the end of the season, he was playing with Kadri and Komarov, ostensibly the Leafs' checking line, the unit spotted against other teams' top lines.

Nikita Zaitsev wound up with 4 goals and 32 assists, leading all league rookies in ice time. For most of the second half, he'd spent great stretches quarterbacking the Leafs' power play, earning him the most total playing time on the team, at least until he went down with injury in Game 82 and was eked out by Jake Gardiner.

Zach Hyman wound up with 10 goals and 18 assists while playing the entire season on Matthews's left wing. As the pro scout noted in the first game in Ottawa, Hyman was useful but not ideally cast as a complement to Matthews—in the second half of the season, it started to look like he'd have to pick up the puck and dive into the net to get something across the goal line. Nonetheless, Hyman's four shorthanded goals were second only to Nashville's Viktor Arvidsson, and he and Komarov were Babcock's first choices on the penalty kill.

The others occasionally made the most of cameo roles. Starting the season with the Marlies and finishing it on the sidelines with injury, Soshnikov didn't put up impressive numbers (5 goals and 4 assists in fifty-six games), but he endeared himself to Babcock with his gritty play. Even better, at twenty-two he had room for growth. Frédérik Gauthier had dressed for twenty-one games and was effective, if not particularly memorable, in his stint. And then there was Kapanen, with his handful of games at season's end and that lone, crucial goal in the late stages of Game 81.

Still, it came back to Matthews, Marner, and Nylander. The Leafs became only the second team in history with three rookies to score at least 60 points. The 1980–81 Quebec Nordiques had done the same with the Stastny brothers—Peter and Anton—and Dale Hunter. But the comparisons ended there. A future Hockey Hall of Famer, Peter Stastny was twenty-four and had a wealth of international experience when he played his first NHL game. His brother, Anton, was twenty-one and similarly seasoned. Hunter had been a couple of months younger than Nylander was when he started his rookie season, but Hunter's 63 points look a lot less impressive than Nylander's and Marner's 61 in the context of league scoring—Connor McDavid led the NHL in scoring with 100 points in 2016–17, but in 1980–81, that would have been good for just thirteenth place.

All told, the eight Leafs rookies put up 304 points across the season. The only group to top that number dated back more than twenty years. Back in the 1992–93 season, the Winnipeg Jets' top five rookies combined for 327 points. That Jets team remains the only one in league history to have four players score 20 goals in their first year. Leading the way was future Hockey Hall of Famer Teemu Selanne, who had one of the greatest runs in NHL history: 76 goals and 132 points in his first season in the league. That, however, shouldn't diminish the balance of the Jets' freshman class, including centre Alexei Zhamnov—who wound up with 25 goals and 72 points that season—and Keith Tkachuk, who scored 28 goals and 51 points (along with 201 penalty minutes) that year and would later score a total of 538 goals in 1,201 career games. The fourth player in the Jets' line-up is the outlier: Evgeny Davydov had 28 goals and 49 points, but that turned out to be his career year; he played the next two seasons with Florida and Ottawa and scored just eight times before heading back to play in various European leagues for the rest of his career. Like with the Stastnys and Hunter in Quebec, the Winnipeg rookies skewed older than the Leafs' rookies: At the start of the 2016–17 season, all three of the Leafs trio were younger than Tkachuk was back in 1992. Tkachuk had been twenty at the start of his rookie season, Selanne and Zhamnov twenty-two, and Davydov twenty-five. And again, like the Nordiques' rookies back in the 1980s, Selanne et al. came along when the scoring rate in the league was a lot higher than it would be in the 2016–17 season.

The historical context and comparisons were background, though. Any dwelling on them would have to wait for the off-season. First, the Leafs had a showdown against the Washington Capitals.

Winners of the Presidents' Trophy for the second year in a row, the Capitals had undergone their tanking and teardown back in the mid-2000s. They'd gone into those drafts with a sharp eye on Europe. They had their own first overall pick in Alexander Ovechkin in 2004; a fourth overall pick two years later in Niklas Backstrom; and, in the years following, an array of highly skilled former first-rounders up front—namely, Marcus Johanssen, André Burakovsky, and Evgeny Kuznetsov. Back on the blueline, they had Dmitry Orlov, a defenceman who had played beside Zaitsev on the Russian team that won the gold at the world juniors in Buffalo. In short, the Capitals had done everything right, with one exception: Even with this core group of players, Washington had never advanced past the second round of the NHL playoffs.

That poor track record had, a couple of seasons earlier, contributed to the firing of George McPhee, the GM who put the pieces in place. The Capitals, by now a mature team, were set on a Cup run. The team had traded for the necessary playoff experience, acquiring former Conn Smythe winner Justin Williams and T. J. Oshie. Braden Holtby ranked as one of the league's top five goaltenders by any measure. The blueline was so deep that their fifth defenceman would almost certainly be on Toronto's top pair. Up front they had an offensive fireworks display. Heading into the playoffs in the spring of 2017, the Capitals seemingly had no weaknesses.

Washington had thumped the Leafs 4–1 at the ACC in the last week of the season, and had done it with absolute impunity—at that point they had already sewn up the Presidents' Trophy and started their backup goalie Philipp Grubauer. Ovechkin's production had dropped significantly—coming off three straight 50-goal seasons, the thirty-one-year-old scored only 33 times, his second-lowest total in a full season in his career. But the stars seemed lined up in Ovechkin's and the Capitals' favour coming into the series against the Leafs, given the absence of Nikita Zaitsev—Ovechkin likely believed that he could feast on Zaitsev and Roman Polak on the right side of the Leafs' blueline, and with Zaitsev out with a concussion, the likes of Martin Marincin and Alexey Marchenko, borderline NHLers at best, would offer all the resistance of speed bumps. That's all the experts figured the Leafs would represent to the Capitals in the first round of the playoffs: an opponent not even requiring a rolling stop.

CHAPTER TWELVE

ON ITS FACE, THE SERIES SHOULDN'T HAVE BEEN A CONTEST.
And after the very first shift of the opening game, that's exactly how
it seemed.

The Leafs were going to have to contend with Alexander Ovechkin and, with Nikita Zaitsev out and Martin Marincin a liability in
nearly every game he had played, they were down to one right-side
option on the blueline for a match-up: Roman Polak. Though virtually every player on each team was nicked up at the end of the season, Polak was almost certainly the furthest from 100 percent—he
hadn't been able to play in the third period of Game 82 after taking a
knee-on-knee hit.

Ovechkin didn't wait at all to send the veteran a message. Off the
opening face-off, with Ovechkin playing beside his linemates Nicklas
Backstrom and T. J. Oshie, the puck drifted into the Toronto end of
the rink, and Ovechkin put Polak in his crosshairs. With a full head
of steam, he leveled Polak, who tried in vain to brace himself. Washington was a "heavy" team—the sort that could exact a heavy physical toll along the boards in the so-called dirty areas of the ice—and
Ovechkin was not just the heaviest on the roster but also arguably
the heaviest in the league, at least among players who bring real skill
to the table. In going after Polak, Ovechkin was taking on not only
the Leafs' preferred match-up but also the only player on Toronto's
roster who reveled in the physical game. Ovechkin's message was

plain—if Polak didn't like it, he should run away. It was a beginning that the Capitals had to like. But within two shifts, it would become clear that the favourites weren't going to be able to bully their way to a sweep. Not even close.

In the third shift of the game, ninety seconds in, Tyler Bozak rushed the puck up the ice on a long three-on-two. Mitch Marner, one of nine Leafs playing in their first NHL playoff game, skated on Bozak's right side, and James van Riemsdyk was on the left. Bozak threw the puck over to JVR, who let loose a shot that Caps goaltender Braden Holtby kicked straight back to him. The Leafs left-winger tried to cash in the rebound, but it hit the post and the puck bounced into the slot. Washington defenceman Brooks Orpik looked for a Leaf crashing the net but didn't see Marner—in fact, Orpik looked right over Marner's head. On his first NHL playoff shift, Marner was skidding on his knees towards the net, but he managed to finish off the shot like he was playing mini sticks on a rec room floor. One-zip Leafs. The goal hit the mute button on the raucous crowd at the Verizon Center.

In the first ten minutes of Game 1, the previously disparaged Leafs exploited glaring holes in the Capitals' game that somehow hadn't been exposed much during the season. As big as the Capitals were, as much as they wanted to intimidate, they couldn't hit what they couldn't catch. In the run-up to Game 1, Mike Babcock spelled out to reporters that he'd tried to impress on his young players that the game in the NHL playoffs was different than the one that they had become accustomed to during the regular season. When asked how it was different, he laid it out in stark terms: "No space. Zero. Battle for every inch of the ice, from the opening face-off to the end."

The coach said that he was at best unconvinced that his message got through to his players. "They're not going to believe me, and then it's going to happen," he said. You can understand if the players didn't buy into any message—if Babcock is anything, it's dramatic. The way he recounted it was as if Babcock had guaranteed death by suffocation, a choke hold around his players' skinny necks. *Everybody get ready for it.*

Babcock might have been sandbagging—it might have been his intention to open the game up all along. Whether it was by his design or happenstance didn't matter. Many on the Washington blueline struggled to keep up with the speedy Toronto forwards—the Presidents' Trophy winners' rear guards were ugly to play against along the wall and in the corners, but on the open ice they couldn't dance with the Leafs. In fact, Toronto's own defencemen recognized that they had an opportunity to take a few liberties, carrying the puck deep into the Washington end.

On just such a sequence, defenceman Jake Gardiner—who was playing the best hockey of his season, maybe his best since his first season in Toronto—went for an extended skate in the Washington end. He skated a full counterclockwise lap, and the Capitals were unable to pin him to the boards or push him off the puck. When he made it to the hash marks on the left wing, he broke for the high slot, pivoting and gliding backwards as the Capitals gave vain chase. Nazem Kadri, the centre that Babcock matched against Backstrom and Ovechkin, as he had against McDavid and other teams' chief offensive threats, stood on the edge of the Washington crease to screen Holtby. Ovechkin backed glutes-first into Kadri, who gave him a hard push in the back. Just as Ovechkin flinched, Gardiner let loose a wrist shot without coming to a stop. Holtby was on the right side of the net, and the puck went to the other side.

A ref immediately waved off the play and, tuning out the Leafs' protests, skated to centre ice, where he turned on his mike. "There's no goal," he said. "The Toronto player was standing right in the middle of the net."

Babcock immediately challenged the call. Only ten times during the season had a play been ruled no-goal on the ice only to be reversed in review. Gardiner's in Game 1 was the eleventh. Kadri had both skates well outside the crease throughout the sequence, which left you wondering exactly what game the ref had been watching.

Things looked rosy for the Leafs, but then came the setbacks. Late in the first period, Brian Boyle was tagged with a minor penalty, a bit of a touch foul, and thirty seconds later, Connor Brown was sent to the box in a case of mistaken identity and a bit of a break, given that the actual culprit was the Leafs' lead choice on the five-on-three penalty kill, Leo Komarov. Ninety tense seconds elapsed, bullets were dodged, and it looked as though the Leafs were going to clear the zone when Justin Williams managed to cut through traffic in front of Andersen to claim a loose puck and beat the goalie.

With four minutes to go in the third period, it was more of the same. Matt Niskanen got a shot off as Matthews dropped to his knee in front of it, just missing the block. Andersen made the initial stop, but the puck dropped right at his feet and he lost it. Williams pounced and poked home another rebound to tie the game.

Williams's two goals laid end to end wouldn't have stretched ten feet. They were all the Capitals could muster in regulation, but they were enough to force overtime.

Babcock had cast forward in the days leading up to the series, talking about what the Leafs were going to look like in two years. He spoke of the Capitals in the most flattering terms, all but saying that they had to rate as the favourites to win the Cup.

The goal in overtime was one of those bolts of lightning that leave you wondering how a game of quality chances ends on a shot that was little more than a hope and a prayer.

Just five or six shifts into extra time, the Capitals' fourth line dumped the puck into the Toronto end. Marincin chased it down and tried to clear the zone past the incoming forechecker, Jay Beagle. The puck didn't make it even halfway up to the blueline. Tom Wilson, a full-grown pest of the first rank, stopped the puck along the boards at the hash mark, and from there, at the farthest point of the right wing and with Rielly bearing down on him, he leaned into a wrist shot. Andersen went down into the butterfly on Wilson's windup, but the puck was headed high-short-side. The goalie managed to get his glove up, but the puck just nicked the webbing and hit the back of the net.

The Capitals poured onto the ice and celebrated while the Leafs cleared the ice. Andersen skated away without a backward look. It had been a winnable game for the Leafs—it certainly looked that way from the first period to well into the third. The Leafs had lost, but still, the game opened more questions than it answered. Was the overtime goal an aberration or the stars lining up? Was it just a poor performance by the Capitals, an overconfident team that was looking beyond the first round? Was it a hint that the Leafs could give them a run? It was going to take more than sixty-three minutes to get comprehensive answers to those questions, but one thing had been established. Contrary to Mike Babcock's warnings, the Leafs had been able to find room enough to breathe out there.

For Jacob Freeman, Saturday, April 15, was an endurance test that Toronto sports fans could only dream about a couple of years ago: back-to-back playoff games for the Raptors and the Maple Leafs, Jurassic Park during the late afternoon and Maple Leaf Square when night fell. Freeman and three friends arrived a half hour before tip-off to take their places at the front of the crowd, right in front of the big screen. It turned out to be good timing, because over the next fifteen minutes, the plaza outside the ACC turned into something like a purple ant colony, a teeming crowd of fans in Raptors merch. Freeman and his cohorts, all college students in Toronto, were in neutral hoodies—it was enough that they were going to stand for seven hours or so, never mind bring a change of outfits. During the Raptors game, Freeman would look out of place in his No. 34 Leafs jersey. Likewise, a satin Raptors jacket with its T. rex would stick out when the cameras panned the crowd during the Leafs game. It wouldn't be as bad as the three Washington fans who had come out in their red Caps sweaters, but still.

Freeman said he and his friends first came out to Maple Leafs Square when they were in grade eleven. "I've seen the video from that playoff game when they lost in Boston with Reimer and the rest," he said. "I didn't come down here. I was probably old enough to do it, but I was wrapped up in other stuff. It's still crazy to see [the video] from that night, though. You can see it on their faces. A real fan knows what it must have felt like to be there that night . . . but if you're not a fan, there's no way that you could know."

Freeman estimated that he and his friends came to "a few games . . . the big ones" over the course of the season, always on Saturday nights: Boston for the home opener, whenever Montreal was on the schedule, the playoff clincher versus Crosby and the Penguins. During the playoffs, though, the day or night of the week didn't matter to them.

"It would be great to be inside the ACC, whichever team, but tickets are just too hard to get and way too expensive for us," Freeman said. "Even going to a sports bar or something like that can get up there [in price]. But this beats watching it at home or going to a friend's place. And really, you might have a better view out here than if you're in the seats up high in the ACC, definitely for the Raptors anyway."

Jurassic Park and Maple Leafs Square are tribal rites, to be sure, and that day you could get a sense of the cultural difference between the tribes—a bit of the irony in that Jurassic Park is very much the New Toronto, a more racially and ethnically diverse crowd, whereas the crowd for the Leafs' game is more Old Toronto, not exclusively the sons and occasional daughters of SCTV's McKenzie Brothers, but well represented. You could pick up common threads, though.

For one thing, the respective crowds were amazingly well behaved. Other than the Sunday crowd outside the pope's window, it's hard to imagine a congregation this size and in such tight quarters in any city without any roiling of tempers. You didn't hear or see anyone complaining about his or her space being invaded. The odd bump in the plaza was just a fact of a fan's life as much as it was for the players on the court and on the ice.

That the crowds were dry, that no one was lugging cases of beer or pulling out mickeys, had a lot to do with ensuring the mostly pleasant disposition. This is probably due to city policing for public drunkenness and anatomical certainties—exactly where in nearby blocks you can find a bathroom that isn't just for customers is a challenge—but more likely it was because there was no getting back to your hard-won spot in the crowd once you left. And these might have been the largest crowds of young people in the city without there being at least a faint whiff of weed. A healthy percentage of any concert crowd would be lit, no doubt. The Raptors and Leafs, no. Nobody came out to "chill." This was all about getting amped up.

If you were at a vantage point in the distance and watched the crowds gather outside the ACC, you didn't need to make out the purple or blue to tell which game the kids on the square were watching. The rhythms of the NBA stand apart from those of the NHL. For hoops, it's sometimes like a drumbeat, probably a function of the twenty-four-second clock, other times like a drumroll when the game opens up and is played on the run. And if a big dunk gets thrown down, a momentary ecstasy washes over the crowd, one that's quickly dialed back for the next possession. By contrast, there's a slow build with hockey. When the Leafs are on a power play, it heightens expectations; on a penalty kill, the anxiety will last a full two minutes. There are also soft spots, though, stretches when one chip-and-chase leads to a clearance, and another chip-and-chase in the other direction produces a line change—you might have a minute pass or even more without any sort of bump in the pulse of the crowd, a steady hum but no crescendo. Jacob Freeman and his friends were looking forward to the emotional roller coaster. They were prepared for a long night, but it went longer than they expected.

After the Raptors dropped their game, virtually all those in Raptors gear cleared out, and the plaza underwent its shift change. By the time the puck dropped, the crowd, now decked out in blue and white, was buzzing. Less than a minute later, the refs' ears would have burned if they could have heard what was yelled at their images on the giant screen. Off the opening face-off, the Capitals' left winger Daniel Winnik, a favourite of Leafs fans for a couple of seasons before being traded to the Caps at the deadline in 2016, gave Roman Polak a shot right in the mush. No call. Then Jake Gardiner, one of the most peace-loving defencemen in the league, was sent to the box for a cross-check on Wilson, the overtime hero from Game 1. It was more of a push than a real blow; it was hard to blame Gardiner, but it was as shaky a start as could be for the Leafs. The Leafs managed to kill off the two minutes, and the early call wasn't bad news for Toronto. If the refs had wanted to establish control of the game early, then Gardiner's penalty had its intended effect—if the Capitals wanted to go for a physical beat-down of the Leafs, they were running the significant risk of putting the best power play in the postseason on the ice. With the home team's heavy game lightened, the Leafs found some room to skate.

Mike Babcock was also able to get match-ups that he wanted, chief among them Nazem Kadri's line out against Nicklas Backstrom's, one that put the Leafs' best defensive winger, Leo Komarov, opposite Alexander Ovechkin. It hasn't always been "as Ovechkin goes, so go the Capitals"—no team can ride one horse to the top of the standings. In fact, with 33 goals across the full schedule, Ovechkin's year marked a steep drop from the 154 goals he had scored over the previous three seasons. The party line in Washington was that Ovechkin had bought into what coach Barry Trotz had been selling—that the Capitals' long-awaited success in the postseason depended on everyone, the franchise player included, buying into a two-way game. Before Trotz arrived in 2014, Ovechkin had a year in which he'd managed to score 51 goals in a season and still wound up with a brutal minus-35 plus/minus rating.

At first glance, Washington's success in the 2017 regular season might have made them seem unstoppable, but there were mixed results to Trotz's supposed retooling of the franchise. From one season to the next, Ovechkin's plus-minus had dropped from plus-21 to plus-6. It was hard to explain. Ovechkin was still playing beside Backstrom, who was thought to be three or four years past his best season. T. J. Oshie had been brought in to add a level of grit and defensive awareness on the right wing. Ovechkin was set up for success, but while the team soared, he for once seemed just a member of the ensemble.

Still, there was no denying the threat Ovechkin posed, and Komarov might have been one of Ovechkin's foremost nemeses. Komarov managed to get Ovechkin off the ice midway through the first period, drawing a holding penalty, but he negated his good work with a bit of theatre that earned a minor for diving. But Ovechkin's penalty seemed to be a play made in frustration, a bit of acting out. Komarov could sit in the box knowing that he'd gotten inside Ovechkin's head.

The crowd out in Maple Leaf Square had reason to roar just before the end of the first period. The play evoked Gardiner's goal in Game 1. The Leafs' defenceman was skating deep into the Caps' zone, going wide. Washington defenceman Matt Niskanen tried to get a stick on Gardiner but ended up dropping his stick and glove and going barehanded, taking on a "Who, me?" expression when it looked like he might be whistled for a holding penalty. The Capitals were scrambling in their end when the puck landed on James van Riemsdyk's stick, and he snapped it by Holtby high on the glove side.

In the second period, it looked like the Leafs were seizing control, but the Capitals scored against the run of play. Boos went up in Maple Leaf Square when the fans saw Ovechkin thrust his arms in the air after a power-play goal four minutes in. The response wasn't quite so strident ten minutes later when defenceman John Carlson stepped in from the blueline and blasted the puck by Andersen. The collective sigh turned to anger seconds later when the camera caught Evgeny Kuznetsov taunting Roman Polak. The Capitals had two goals on only three shots in the period.

There was worse to come. A couple of shifts later, the hundreds of fans cringed as one when Brooks Orpik dealt a heavy check to Polak, and the Leafs' defenceman folded under him at a gruesome angle. "I can't watch that stuff," Jacob Freeman said. It was clear on impact that Polak was done for the series and then some. Toronto's blueline had been a known weakness all season, one that you'd have imagined the Leafs would have addressed at the trading deadline. The Leafs were going to have to go with five defencemen for the rest of the game, as they were already playing without Nikita Zaitsev, who was still out with a suspected concussion. It looked grim for any comeback and for stretching the series beyond four games.

The Leafs clearly didn't see it that way, though. Just a few shifts after Polak went down, Kasperi Kapanen tied the game on a slick finish off a feed from Matt Martin. Kapanen was stationed in the slot with his back to Holtby when Martin slid him the puck through traffic. Kapenen coolly controlled it and then spun around, finding the five-hole with a backhand. Kapanen exulted, but it looked like it might have been premature—Barry Trotz called for a review, believing that Martin had been offside when he skated into the Capitals' end.

Out on Maple Leafs Square, the wait was excruciating. Each angle on the replay showed Martin's back skate was on the blueline by an inch, at most. That is, of course, unless he lifted his heel—if the refs judged Martin had broken contact with the ice, then the goal would have to be waved off. The camera angle zoomed in so tight that the image of Martin's skate was bigger than a tractor trailer on the screen. Finally, the ref took off his headset. There was a moment of absolute stillness, and then the crowd erupted as the ref pointed to centre ice. The goal stood up.

And the Leafs weren't done there. Morgan Rielly restored the Leafs' lead on a shot from the point on a power play with thirteen seconds left in the second period. Holtby had no chance on it. Orpik, Carlson, and Beagle were all standing in the goaltender's sight line, as were Matthews and van Riemsdyk. Holtby leaned one way, and the puck went the other into a half-open net. The lead looked like it was going to stand up until late in the third, when Backstrom tied it up, sending the game into overtime and Jacob Freeman and friends into a seventh hour in the elements.

Freeman had to make his case to his friends, who debated how long they'd be willing to wait. "It will be over fast like the other night," he assured them. Famous last words.

Many an overtime turns into a cautious grind, but not this one. Both teams had potential heroes waiting in the wings. For Washington, you would have thought it would be Ovechkin to step up—it was hard to figure Barry Trotz's thinking, but his star had played under sixteen minutes in regulation. In the overtime period, the camera occasionally caught Ovechkin lobbying Trotz for ice time. For the Leafs, you might have imagined it would be Auston Matthews—his line had been driving possession effectively in the first period but hadn't had an impact on the scoresheet yet.

But instead of the stars, it was a couple of the least-likely players on the ice who would put an end to the night.

For one moment, it looked like it would be Zach Hyman, whose struggles to score on Matthews's wing had been a sore point in fan forums since January. Midway through the first overtime, Hyman was out at the end of a long shift on a penalty kill when the Caps turned the puck over, freeing the rookie for a breakaway. They had to have been the longest 120 feet of Hyman's life. He bore down on Holtby, but before he could get a shot off or try a deke, Carlson closed the distance and got a stick on him. Carlson was risking a penalty or even a penalty shot, but he wasn't whistled, and an exhausted Hyman tumbled into Holtby and the net, knocking it off the magnets. When Hyman got back up on his skates, it looked as though he couldn't remember exactly where he left his legs, and he looked as tired as everyone standing in Maple Leaf Square.

The crowd was thinning, and those who remained were filled with dread when Ovechkin had a breakaway of his own with seconds left in the period. As Andersen turned aside Ovechkin's deke, the crowd responded with the most full-throated shouts of the night.

Jacob Freeman stuck around for the second overtime. His friends had gone home, and he considered joining them. He had talked himself into the idea that if a goal didn't come quickly in one overtime, it would in the next. As the second overtime began, he hoped his faith would be repaid.

The Leafs' fourth-liners had taken the loss in Game 1 hardest among their teammates. They were supposed to grind away and shut things down, but they had been on the ice for two of Washington's goals, including Wilson's overtime winner. Kapanen's goal in the second period had more than given them a lift, but it was nothing like what happened eight minutes into the second overtime.

It wasn't the sort of sequence that Babcock would draw up on an erasable board. The fourth-liners were out for a face-off in the Capitals' end when centre Brian Boyle was thrown out of the circle and Kapanen stepped into his place. An exchange of Boyle, a powerful six-foot-six veteran who's excellent on the draw, for Kapanen, a kid who plays the wing; the fourth line out there—it didn't look like the beginning of a magic moment. But Kapanen won the face-off from Kuznetsov, and he and his fellow fourth-liners controlled the puck on the cycle. Then John Carlson broke his stick, and immediately the Caps were scrambling. Boyle started rounding clockwise behind the net—never fleet of foot, he took off with more of a lumber than a burst of speed. It looked like he was going for a wraparound on Holtby, who hugged his left post. Boyle either sensed that Kapanen had shaken Carlson or caught the rookie at the open side of the net in his peripheral vision. A behind-the-back pass gave Kapanen a clean look and an easy finish for his second goal of the game and the third of his NHL career.

Jacob Freeman and the rest of the fans who'd remained in Maple Leaf Square erupted into cheers. Their patience had been rewarded in the most dramatic fashion. It was just before midnight when Freeman finally started to make his way home, drinking in the night. The Leafs had won, the series was tied, and the team was coming home. It was sweet relief on more than one front. "I was worried that if it went to another overtime, the subway was going to close," he said.

CHAPTER THIRTEEN

YOU HAD TO IMAGINE THAT ALEXANDER OVECHKIN WAS OPER-
ating on a few things when he took a run at Nikita Zaitsev off the
opening face-off in Game 3: the message delivered by Barry Trotz,
the scouting report intel, his own impulses. Zaitsev had missed
the first two games in the series with what the team termed an "an
upper-body injury," an injury that, after reviewing the hit he ab-
sorbed in the Columbus game, you presumed to be a concussion.
Zaitsev was returning to fill the void left by the loss of Polak, a trade-
off that marked a big uptick in puck skills and an equal markdown in
physical pushback. Ovechkin wanted to set his terms early.

Matt Niskanen followed Ovechkin's lead after a stoppage in play
in front of Holtby's net a couple of shifts later. Niskanen targeted another perceived weak link, a playoff neophyte who could be intimi-
dated, when he dropped Mitch Marner with a gloved fist to the face
in the middle of a scrum in front of Holtby's net five seconds after a
whistled stoppage. The idea that Marner was somehow taking liberties with Holtby was laughable, but the situation offered Niskanen
just enough justification to escape without a penalty. Marner went
down like he had fainted.

Though the Leafs had staged a mighty upset in Game 2 and
played well enough to win the opener, they were reeling in the first
playoff game at the ACC in four years. The new management's vision for the team of the future was being put to the test—other than

Zach Hyman, all the young players brought in were long on skill but hardly gloried in a physical game. They wanted to dance rather than wrestle, while the Capitals could do both. In fact, Washington was a team in the profile that Brian Burke had desired—skilled and, yes, truculent, and all the word's five-dollar synonyms.

The strategy of putting the Leafs back on their heels paid off early. The Capitals ran out to a 2–0 lead before the ice was scarred up. Both goals came from Washington's first line, Backstrom scoring on the first shot on Frederik Andersen, Ovechkin on the second. On Backstrom's goal, Zaitsev got his wires crossed in coverage with James van Riemsdyk. On Ovechkin's, well, it was what the Leafs had seen on video and what fans had seen for more than a decade— a one-time blast from his office, the circle on the left wing. The Capitals were rolling, and just a few minutes into the game, the Leafs were trying to hold on and stop the bleeding.

Then, just past the midway point of the first period, came an unlikely turn. The Leafs, punching way over their weight class, pushed back against the bullies. It wasn't the rookies who stepped up. That wasn't in their profiles, or their job descriptions. It fell to the checking line, the two nastiest forwards of the Leafs' top three lines: Nazem Kadri and Leo Komarov. And they sent the message in the most compelling way, going right after those who were out to intimidate the young Leafs.

For all the criticisms leveled against Kadri, no one ever accused him of playing scared. He might only have been a middleweight by league standards, but he played the body stealthily—not every shift, not recklessly, but when an opponent was most exposed and didn't see it coming. Along the wall in the Capitals' end, Kadri dropped Orpik, who had taken out Polak and nearly done the same with Marner in Game 2. Kadri crushed the Capitals' defenceman, who had to take a breath before getting back up on his skates. Then, seconds later on the same shift, Komarov laid into Ovechkin. The two hits flipped a switch and dialed up the Leafs' work rate for the rest of the period.

It paid off. Late in the first period, Kadri leveled Orpik with a second massive hit. The play allowed Toronto to recover the puck in their end, and then Matthews went to work, rushing up the middle, looking to split two Capitals defencemen. When it seemed to him that he had no daylight, he let fly a shot in full stride from just inside the blueline. The puck caromed off Nate Schmidt's upper body—it was hard to tell if the puck hit Schmidt just below his neck or in fact bounced off his chin—but it dropped with a thud, and Matthews had anticipated exactly where it would land. He blew by Schmidt and bore in on Holtby, deking him with a move that was hard to follow even on the slow-motion replay.

Given the Leafs' shaky start, it seemed like they had weathered the worst of the storm, going into the first intermission down only a goal. But the Capitals weren't done.

Five minutes into the second period, Washington was back in front by two after a goal by Evgeny Kuznetsov, who knocked home a rebound of a shot by Marcus Johansson. That was only the start of the trouble. A couple of shifts later, Leafs defenceman Matt Hunwick was whistled for a hooking penalty, and in the ensuing scrum Matt Martin tangled with Tom Wilson. It wasn't immediately clear who instigated the dance, but one of the refs believed it to be Martin and gave him a double minor. So the Capitals had a full, two-minute five-on-three power play, more than enough room for Backstrom and Ovechkin to operate and give the Caps a commanding lead. With great work by Rielly, Komarov, and Hyman, and something less than maximum urgency by Washington, the Capitals squandered the opportunity.

When the penalties expired, Marner (who had been in the box, serving the first of Martin's two penalties) stepped out of the box just as the puck had been shot up the ice and cleared the Capitals' last man back; Marner had nothing but ice between him and the net, if he could just beat Holtby to the puck. The Caps goalie sprinted out of his net and got there first by a split second, sliding skates-first and knocking the puck away with his stick as Marner went flying. Still, once again the Leafs had to feel like they were leading a charmed life—they had a better scoring chance on the penalty kill than any generated by the Caps' five-on-three.

With renewed energy, the Leafs went to work. With about five minutes to go in the second period, Brown was standing in front of Holtby, fighting off Orpik, when Kadri let go a shot from midrange. Brown managed to get a stick on the puck, which also seemed to bounce off the seat of Orpik's hockey pants. Holtby had no chance. Their third goal showed Matthews's line to full effect. Again it was Orpik who was the butt of the sequence. On a shoot-in, Hyman knocked Orpik off the puck, and Matthews retrieved it before flipping a backhand pass to Nylander, who was alone in front of the net. Nylander got off one shot that Holtby stopped, but, just as Nylander controlled the rebound, forward André Burakovsky made a desperate attempt to knock the puck off his stick. For all his late back-checking urgency, Burakovsky landed squarely on top of his goaltender, and any slim chance Holtby had of making a second save was gone.

Things had mostly gone the Capitals' way, and yet the game was tied. It seemed the Leafs' team speed was going to be the antidote for Washington's heavy game. Through the last twenty minutes of regulation, it was the Capitals who were lucky to remain tied—they didn't register a shot through the first thirteen minutes of the third period, and the likes of Orpik and others weren't getting any fleeter in pursuit of the Leafs' forwards. Even into the last minute of regulation, everything was trending Toronto's way, and with the home team threatening, Washington's Lars Eller was given a minor for high-sticking.

Toronto's ensuing man advantage might have allowed them to end the game right there, but the horn blew. For the third straight game, overtime would be needed to decide things. Toronto would be on the power play at the start of the sixty-first minute. Eller stepped out of the box and skated directly to the bench to take a long walk to the dressing room.

Rookies had accounted for all the Leafs' goals to this point, but it was two veterans who authored the game winner. Kadri was stationed on the sideboards and found Bozak with a hard pass in the slot. Bozak didn't stop the puck or one-time it, but instead simply deflected it artfully. Neither Holtby or anybody else could have reacted quickly enough to get in front of it. Like those that followed Kapanen's and Brown's goals in Game 81, the cheers that went up after Bozak's game winner were so loud that fans hardly needed the horn and the flashing exhortations on the big screen. This wasn't just a cheer. This was catharsis.

In the Washington dressing room after the game, the team was in denial. Ovechkin told reporters that he wasn't too concerned being down two games to one to a team loaded with playoff neophytes.

"Just forget [Game 3] and move forward," Ovechkin said. "Obviously, we're losing the series, but it's not over yet. We should have won this game, but we made a couple of mistakes with a couple of unlucky bounces. But that's the game. You move forward."

The opening of Game 4 was almost a perfect match to the sequence two nights earlier, with the opening momentum coming entirely in Washington's favour, and entirely on the sticks of the Capitals'

first-liners. Fans were still finding their seats when T. J. Oshie opened
the scoring three minutes in, and, three shifts later, Ovechkin blasted
another one-time slap shot from the left side.

Also for the second game in a row, the Leafs drew back within a
goal, taking less than a minute to respond to Ovechkin's laser. Zach
Hyman was credited with the goal, but all the work had been done
by Nylander, who had carried the puck through the Capitals' zone,
fending off Dmitry Orlov and Tom Wilson before finding Jake Gardiner briefly open on the blueline. Gardiner was stumbling when he
let loose a shot, and it took a magic-bullet path, deflecting off first
Hyman's skate and then Niskanen's before going past Holtby.

All that, though, set the stage for a moment that turned the
course of the series on a dime. When the story of this game is told
down the line, it will not be Ovechkin's shining moment, nor that
of any of Washington's shining stars, but rather Tom Wilson, a Toronto native who grew up playing for Don Mills a few years before
Mitch Marner landed in the organization. He was a hometown boy,
a grinder, a twenty-three-year-old who had made the Capitals team
three seasons ago mostly on nerve and the willingness to do some
awful things. He was the one who scored in overtime in Game 1
and who swung Game 3 on a single shift—preventing one goal in
the Washington end, then scoring a back-breaking goal on Frederik
Andersen.

It looked like the Leafs were going to tie the game fourteen minutes in when Morgan Rielly skated in from the point and let fly a shot
that key-punched a new five-hole between Holtby's pads. The goaltender didn't quite stop the puck, but he slowed it to a crawl. He could
see it rolling slowly behind him towards the goal line, but not in time
to reach back for it. Enter Wilson. He dived headfirst into the net and
swatted the puck away with a couple of inches to spare. While play
went on, Wilson gathered himself and got back to his skates without

dislodging the Washington net from its magnets—a seemingly small detail in this sequence but one that made a huge difference.

Back on his skates, Wilson joined the play heading south to the Leafs' end. Lars Eller let loose a shot, and when Andersen couldn't control the rebound, Wilson was standing there behind Rielly, ready to bury the puck. Wilson had not only prevented the game from being tied two-all but he'd almost single-handedly made it 3–1.

On his very next shift, Wilson laid a heavy check on Rielly, who went down hard and whose lip caught the skate blade of Burakovsky—Rielly was lucky to need only a couple of stiches. With Rielly dazed and getting back on his skates, Burakovsky and Wilson took off on a two-on-one with only Matt Hunwick to face them, and they made no mistakes. Wilson had his second of the game. By the end of the period, the Capitals had outshot the home team 15–6. The favourites had their best period of the series when they needed it most.

Entering the second period trailing by three goals, the Leafs were down, but they weren't out. Not yet. James van Riemsdyk would score in the second period, but Oshie would answer with another for Washington, and it was still a three-goal margin going into the third. More than that, though, the Capitals drove possession in the Leafs' end for shifts at a time.

The Leafs tried to rally in the third. They had outshot the Capitals 14–1 through to seven minutes left in regulation when a Rielly shot was blocked by Orpik and went right to Matthews, who put the puck into a wide-open net. Bozak then scored with about half a minute to go, which made the final score 5–4, which looked closer than the game did to the eyes of those watching and playing in it.

Mike Babcock didn't spin it. He said that his team had a tougher issue dealing with prosperity than adversity, that Game 3 had made them ripe for the picking.

"One team relaxes and feels pretty good about themselves," he said. "They all tell you how great they're doing, while the other team gets prepared."

It might have been harsh, but it was honest—Babcock's team had thoroughly dominated the Capitals in the third period in Game 3 but showed up a half hour late two nights later. They might have thought that they had been the better team through four games, but all they had to show for it were two wins and exceeded expectations.

"It was clean, *clean,*" Dave Pal said as he looked up at the big screen in TKO's and saw Nazem Kadri skating towards the penalty box, making his case to the zebra.

Less than a minute before in real time, with a little over two minutes left in the first period of Game 5, Kadri had thrown a hip check into Ovechkin at the Washington blueline. Ovechkin had been in full flight going down the left wing, looking to skate around Kadri until the centre had lined him up. The crowd at TKO's had cheered on impact and roared even more when Ovechkin stayed down on the ice after he'd tried and given up getting back up on his skates under his own power. As the trainer made his way onto the ice to attend to the Capitals' star, the *Hockey Night in Canada* crew replayed the hit, and it was clear that Ovechkin's knee was hyperextended. For all the full-on forty-foot runs Ovechkin had taken at Toronto defencemen, including a crushing check early in the game on Jake Gardiner, the knockout blow had been laid on Ovechkin by a centre who was giving away thirty, maybe forty pounds, who had once been a lightning rod for Leafs fans' vitriol, and who had put together an outstanding season, scoring a career-high 32 goals and facing other teams' top lines, all while overshadowed by the exploits of Matthews, Marner, and Nylander.

The Capitals wanted the refs to give Kadri a major and toss him from the game for a deliberate (not to mention successful) attempt to injure, but they would get neither. Dave Pal and everyone at the bar said it was just an old-fashioned hip check. "They're turning the NHL into the No Hitting League," Pal said. "Kadri caught him, that's all."

When Don Cherry came on in the first intermission and the hit was replayed in "Coach's Corner," the TV personality seconded the motion.

"It's a beauty . . . remember Leo Boivin," Cherry would say, citing a Hall of Fame defenceman who was the master of the open-ice hip check, an art form as archaic as cursive handwriting. "If there's an injury, they look for a penalty."

It looked like Kadri had leveled the blow that would define the series. And it did have a big impact on the game, just not in the way that he or the Leafs or the fans at TKO's and sports bars across the city imagined. Kadri was handed only a minor for tripping on the hit, and while he was in the box, Oshie scored on a power play to give the Capitals a 1–0 lead at the end of the first period.

The Leafs were probably a bit unlucky to come out of the period down a goal. In contrast to their two home games, the Leafs had gotten off to a quick start. Twenty seconds into the game, Connor Brown and Leo Komarov had a two-on-one with the Caps' Nate Schmidt back. Brown threaded a pass to the left-winger and forced Holtby to make a tough glove save. Through their first three or four shifts, the line of Matthews, Nylander, and Hyman exerted heavy pressure and sustained possession in the Washington end. They gave as good as they got through twenty minutes, but there was nothing on the scoreboard to show for it.

Ovechkin missed the remaining minutes of the first period after Kadri laid the hip on him, but he was back for the second period.

Then the game took a decidedly ugly turn. Ovechkin speared Kadri with no call, and a few minutes later, Niskanen slashed Kadri across the back of his right knee, a home-run swing that earned Niskanen two minutes in the penalty box. Then Ovechkin stapled Gardiner once again into the boards. Matt Martin, the tough guy on the fourth line, tried to respond in kind, which caused Dave Pal some despair.

"They just don't have anyone on their top three lines who can take care of that stuff for them," Pal said. "You know, those teams that Pat Quinn had back then [in the early 2000s], they had those guys—Roberts, Tucker, Domi, Corson. Other than Domi, those other guys were on your top three lines—they helped you, could get goals. Maybe [those Quinn teams] didn't have enough skilled guys. If it's Kadri and Uncle Leo [Komarov] who have to try to be the physical guys up front, it's asking them to do something that they're not really made for. It's not enough."

Despite the Leafs' disadvantage in this department, they had a chance to again take a lead in the series, but their power play, the best of any team's in the playoffs, couldn't generate much in the way of quality chances: They mustered a total of only four shots on four trips with the man advantage.

Matthews tied the game six minutes into the second period. With Hyman again occupying Holtby and the Capitals defencemen in front of the net, Matthews cashed in a rebound of a rebound after a shot by Nylander.

The game stayed tied at one through to the end of regulation, largely in part to what were probably the best performances by both Andersen and Holtby in the series. The patrons at TKO's held their places, held on to hope, and held their breath until the refs blew their whistles for stoppages. For the fourth time in five games, the match stretched into overtime.

"It's right there with '93," Pal said in the intermission before overtime. "The thing is, even before they play the seven games against Gretzky and L.A., they're life-or-death against St. Louis—that goal in double OT by Gilmour [against the Blues] was really the biggest moment of that whole season. This isn't '93, not quite, but it's different. That team in '93 had all kinds of players. . . . They were supposed to have a shot . . . it was supposed to be their year. Nobody thought anything like that with this team, though. Next year isn't even their year, really, and maybe not the year after that. It's a shock that they're doing what they're doing. Other teams have those miracle runs. . . . For once it's us."

The Leafs were one miracle short, though. The patrons at TKO's ordered beers and Dave Pal freshened his soda water, digging in for a long overtime. "It could go two," one patron said. It wound up not even lasting two whole shifts. Justin Williams, aka Mr. Game 7, the renowned clutch goal scorer, finished off a setup from Marcus Johansson sixty-four seconds into the frame. When he did, shoulders sagged the length of the bar, as if choreographed.

Within two minutes, Pal looked to the immediate future. "They can still stretch it to seven games, I think," he said.

Two minutes after that, he looked to a future beyond that. "You know, a guy like Williams, he'd be a good add at the right price," he said.

I won't hazard a guess how many Leafs games I've watched from the stands or the press box in my life. The first was in standing room with my father at Maple Leaf Gardens. I was seven, turning eight, which meant I had to stand on my toes for sixty minutes of stop time to peer over the heads of the people seated in the blues. The Bruins were in town, and it was the season before Bobby Orr landed in Boston. Back in those days, the Bruins were the sixth of the Original Six, and the Leafs were contenders; the line-up included most of those who would go on to win the Cup in 1967.

I ran the gamut in the decades since, luckily never having to stand all night. I made it to a few games at the Gardens in cheap seats during the 1970s. In the eighties, when I worked on the Leafs program for a stretch, I was up in a private box a handful of nights. By the nineties I was up on press row, where I remained from mid-decade on, including the closing of the Gardens and the opening of the Air Canada Centre.

Keon, Sittler, McDonald, Salming, Clark, Gilmour, Sundin: I was lucky enough to see all of them play in person, although my timing could have been slightly better. I missed a lot of the landmark games: Sittler's 10-point night; the upset of the Islanders back in 1978; the thrilling run in 1993. But Game 6 against the Capitals will take its own place in my memories.

You get to a certain age and you can't resist saying that you've seen it all before. It's almost reflexive to say, "It was better back then." This time, though, it wasn't. I'm not hidebound, clinging to what was. I'm one of those who believe that those from today would beat those from yesterday, that when the game evolves it improves, that there's more skill and speed on the ice now than there was then. Some will say that history's great players would still stand out in today's NHL, and I'll give that a lukewarm endorsement. I'll always counter by suggesting that a middle-rank player today would tear it up if he could travel back in time to the 1960s or '70s.

At the highest moments in Game 6, I heard cheers rise up in the ACC unlike any others I experienced at a Leafs game. When it looked like the Leafs might improbably win, I heard a cheer that came from somewhere deep down, prayers answered. Pinch me. Maybe this time it's us. When the reality of defeat set in, the cheer came from somewhere else, imagination dancing. How good it will be when it happens. And it will happen.

It was a tense affair for forty-eight minutes, a goalless tie, and the nineteen thousand at the ACC turned from jubilant at the start of the game to nervous by the third period. They were seized by a collective dread that this small miracle of a season might be at an end. While the Leafs had sustained pressure and cycled the puck in the Capitals' end for stretches, Washington's forwards generated the most chances. They pounced on breakdowns in the home team's end. Somehow the shots favoured the Leafs through to the end of the third period, 37 to 31. It didn't matter, though—the quality chances were three to one, maybe more, for the Capitals. Only Frederik Andersen kept the game from being a rout. In fact, in overtime, the Leafs would be able to muster only one shot on Holtby, off the stick of Connor Brown, and couldn't generate any quality scoring chances.

It wasn't the season in microcosm, not a wholly representative look at the team. If you had never watched the Leafs until Game 6 of this series with the Presidents' Trophy winner and were told that three of its first-year players were the talk of the league, you might have wondered exactly which three were the breakthrough players. Matthews would have been the only truly obvious one, although he'd had many better games. Nylander struggled somewhat, Marner more so. Zaitsev was less than 100 percent. Hyman and Kapanen excelled—no one was more industrious than the former, no one moved around faster than the latter.

It's not forcing symmetry for the sake of narrative to say that the Leafs' season ended as it started. In Ottawa, Matthews had scored the team's first four goals of the season in a loss in overtime to the Sens. In Games 5 and 6 against Washington, he scored the team's last two goals of the season in a pair of overtime losses to the Capitals. In both the first game of the season and the last game of the playoff run, he was on the ice when the game was lost. In Ottawa in October, Matthews tested the fans' credulity with every passing minute, but by April everyone in the building—teammates, coaches, and fans— was looking at him, waiting, hoping, and, yes, expecting. The goal that was needed most was likeliest to come from him. It didn't need to have the sublime skill of that second goal in Ottawa. As far as the fans were concerned, any old goal would do.

The sequence started with Rielly hammering the puck into the right-wing corner of the Capitals' end. For the world, it looked like a generic dump-in leading to a chase along the wall and scrums for possession. Thus did Matt Niskanen and Dmitry Orlov wheel back towards their respective corners. Into the great void in the middle of the ice Matthews skated, an exploratory forecheck.

Which is to say, nobody on the ice or in the arena could have predicted what was going to happen just a couple of seconds later.

It was unclear how the puck caromed out of the corner and directly to Matthews in the slot, with no defender within yards of him. After a hundred replays in the coming days, there would still be no telling how it happened. Some thought the puck hit a stanchion. Others thought it ricocheted off a seam in the gate where the arena crew comes out. Someone on press row thought it might have hit a small porthole in the glass where the photogs position their telephoto lenses. From directly across the rink and high above, it looked as though it went off the rink board ad for Planters' Peanuts—yes, banking off Mr. Peanut, off his top hat or cane or monocle.

However the puck landed on Matthews's stick, it couldn't have been any cleaner or crisper if it had been Nylander feeding him the puck on an open sheet in practice. Matthews instantly reacted to this puck from seemingly out of nowhere and brought it under control without the slightest stutter. On his first touch, in tight quarters, Matthews put it into the back of the top corner past Holtby's waving glove.

When the celebration started on the ice, fans in the stands entertained the idea that the Leafs could extend the series to a seventh game. They might even have wondered about seeing the team back again in a second series against Pittsburgh. It would be Game 81 all over again. That was getting far too ahead of themselves, though. That was going somewhere that would never come to be.

From Matthews's goal on, it was all Caps, all the way. They smothered the Leafs, who really didn't get another scoring chance. Somehow, though, the Leafs held up and managed to extend the game to overtime for the fifth out of six games. It seemed that there might be some magic left after all.

There was, but it was the Capitals who would channel it. It wasn't the most likely candidates who led the way for Washington—not Ovechkin, not his centre Backstrom. Backstrom had his usual game, but Ovechkin had something less. He didn't have the same burst in his skating—clearly, he was still feeling the effects of the hip check that Nazem Kadri dropped on him in Game 5.

Instead, it was Marcus Johansson. He and his linemates, Evgeny Kuznetsov and Justin Williams, had been consistently dangerous throughout the entire game, scoring the tying goal late in the third period. You expected Williams, with his three Stanley Cup rings and a Conn Smythe Trophy, to have an impact in the series, and sure enough, he factored into the end of the Leafs' season. Just over six minutes into the extra frame, with the Capitals controlling the play in the Leafs' end, Williams fired a shot from the right hash marks on net. Andersen made the save, but the puck bounced to Johansson right in from of him. Johansson shoveled the puck towards the net, and a sprawling Andersen watched as it bounced past him, carrying the last of Toronto's playoff hopes with it.

Not one fan left the building while the teams filed by each other in the handshake line. After the last of the Capitals had stepped off the ice and headed to the visitors' dressing room, the Leafs stood at centre ice and raised their sticks, one last salute to their crowd. Then a cheer went up that made the skin tingle, a cheer that was an expression of thanks and hope, for what was, what the city had been given, and what would be.

More than a few dressing rooms after a loss are filled with tears and anger. Not on this night. Matthews was far from nonchalant about his season's end, but he didn't have to try hard to see the big picture. This season had been satisfying as it had rolled out, but it foreshadowed far more to come down the line.

"[Losing] is not the best feeling, but if you look around in the room, I think we gave our all," said Matthews. "I think we left it all on the ice. And I think we have a bright future. The experience itself, it's hard, grinding hockey against the best team in the league. I think we gave them all they could handle. We can hold our heads up high. It's not the best feeling, but we can be proud."

EPILOGUE

THE PLAYERS' EXIT INTERVIEWS WITH MANAGEMENT WERE scheduled for Tuesday, April 25, the day before given over to a period of mourning. Along with those meetings came the other ritual that accompanies the NHL giving way to summer: locker clean-out. There was a time when players would actually physically pack up their skates, sticks, and equipment, but those days are long gone. The stalls were all but completely emptied already when the players arrived. It was simply stage management, the pretense for the players' one-on-ones with team officials and the media.

Less than forty-eight hours had passed since Johansson's overtime goal, and the loss in Game 6 was still fresh. The handshake line and the stick-raised wave to the crowd could have served as a last and lasting impression of this strange and wonderful season. What had happened on the ice needed no further explanation, you might have thought. There was no sense in raking the coals that had just gone cold. Nothing had changed since game's end, and there was nothing more to add.

I've been in more than a few of these sessions, and they are a mixed bag. When the season has been a death march that fell short of the playoffs, not a few players have to feign disappointment when, really, resignation set in long before, and it's relief they feel at everything being over. When a team had a shot at going deep and maybe winning it all, the honest workers have to throw out "That's hockey" or some other empty line to minimize their profound disappointment.

By many measures, the Maple Leafs' season had been unlike any other, and so it stood to reason that the postscript would be the same. The dressing room to which the team had retreated after Game 6 was, just thirty-six hours later, strangely upbeat. The players had somehow already placed their accomplishments in perspective: A team with six rookies had taken just about the full measure of the Presidents' Trophy winners.

When security opened the dressing room door for reporters, only one Leaf was sitting at his stall: James van Riemsdyk, a holdover from the Burke era and the Game 7 loss in Boston. If you were looking for someone to define the arc of this team over the past five years, then van Riemsdyk would have had a good perspective.

"You can sense the direction now," he said. "It's clear what we're going to do here. It's fun when you're winning games and in the mix." Which probably is to say, in previous years, van Riemsdyk and other veterans, however earnestly they might have worked, couldn't sense a direction, had no idea what the plan was, and found it anything but fun to be around a league doormat.

If, however, you were looking for someone to look ahead, then perhaps the twenty-seven-year-old wasn't the best in the room to offer comment. Even at that young age, his future wasn't likely the team's, at least not in an all-encompassing sense. He had just wrapped the penultimate season in a six-year, $25.5 million deal that he had signed in Philadelphia before Brian Burke traded for him. His name had already been tossed around in trade rumours in midwinter. Even if the team wanted to extend JVR's contract, the odds seemed long, as his contract renewal would happen at the same time that the likes of Matthews, Marner, and Nylander were hitting their primes as players.

The next player to walk into the room and hold court was

Morgan Rielly. He took a place in the centre of the room rather than at his stall, to accommodate a larger scrum of reporters and cameras. He wasn't the "generational player" on the team, but he was the spokesman of his generation, and not simply because he was practiced in dealing with the media. The unbandaged cuts on his face and across the bridge of his nose were spring's badges of honour and working metaphors for the three seasons prior to this one, when the Maple Leafs took beatings on and off the ice.

"You look at where we were at last season and where we are now, it's a big change," Rielly said. "But like I've said before, it's just one step in the right direction, that's all. We have bigger things we want to achieve. We've grown together, matured and improved. Your goal is to come to the rink each day and improve. I have a lot of work left to do. I think we all do."

A few minutes later, Auston Matthews arrived and took his place at one end of the room, where a wide high-def video display was set to a default Maple Leafs logo. He assumed a casual stance, leaning up against a counter while reporters crowded him. He glanced down at the mikes thrust inches from his chin and then looked up. He wore a gray Leafs hoodie and hadn't bothered to tie up his blue Nike high-tops. When asked about lessons he had drawn from the season, Matthews went to the broad strokes. "You learn as you go," he said. "Pretty veteran guys in here, guys who have been around for a while. It's a long season. I'm exhausted. It's been a grind."

Matthews did have one piece of news to break, and it went directly to the idea of the season as a grind: He was going home to Arizona and passing up an invitation to play for the United States at the world championships.

"I talked it over with my agent and my family," he said. "[It was discussed] in my exit interview. It's just been kind of nonstop this year."

The dots were easy to connect, and the reasoning was sound.

Matthews's season had started back at the start of September, when he had reported to play for Team North America at the World Cup; he hadn't missed a regular-season or playoff game, and he had played in the All-Star Game. The team had leaned on him in the stretch, as well as in the six games every other night. Because of the auspicious start, it might have seemed like there was no learning curve for Matthews, but there surely was—he'd had two long stretches when he couldn't find the back of the net. Next season with the Maple Leafs was his paramount interest. Maybe there would have been a case to make for the worlds if he hadn't already played and starred in the world championships last year. He also might have made the case that it would be a worthwhile trip if the NHL was planning to participate in the Olympics—those who want consideration for selection to the Olympic teams know that their national federations favour those who give up a couple of weeks of their springs to play in the worlds. With the NHL pulling out of the Winter Games in South Korea in 2018, though, it was hard to make a compelling case to go.

Mitch Marner was going to go to the worlds, however. When he arrived at his stall, he was wearing a Jays ball cap with an oversize bill and a look that was basically bemused chill. A television reporter, not one who covers the Leafs, walked up to Marner and, in arch-dramatic fashion, said: "Mitch, it's over. Was it worth it? Did you miss out on anything?" She then thrust the microphone in front of him. It's not clear if the camera picked up his you-got-to-be-kidding-me expression, but his eye-roll would have been loud enough to register on the mike. "Miss out? Maybe a couple of birthdays or something. I'm not too sure. I'm from this area, so I'm pretty close if I want to do something with my family."

Of course it wasn't "over." It was only starting. Mitch Marner and his family might have given up a couple of things along the way, but he couldn't think of anything on the spot. This had always been the plan.

Asked if he was proud of what he accomplished, Marner made a neat deflection, as though he were parked at the edge of the crease, waving his stick at a shot from the point. "It's been pretty cool. It wouldn't have happened without the other guys in this locker room. They've helped me out a lot all season long and made me a better player."

Humility aside, Marner's confidence had allowed him to keep any doubt in check along the way. "You just have to believe in yourself," he said. "Playing with the same guys all season long helped. You develop chemistry that way."

When William Nylander emerged wearing a gaudy Raptors ball cap to offset Marner's lid, the same television reporter chased him down and, though she didn't start with "It's over," asked again, "Was it was worth it?" As if that were the sum total of all the season would be.

Nylander suppressed any disbelief at the question. "Of course it was worth it," he said. "We all love what we do."

A self-assessment is always part of the exit interviews with management, a simple measure of a player's understanding of and honesty about his place in the mix and the state of his game—in the context of the employer-employee debrief, such individual insights are the point of the exercise.

But things are different with the media. In front of reporters for the last time before going home to Sweden to be with his family, Nylander eschewed the first-person singular for the first-person plural when asked about progress. Still days away from turning twenty-one, Nylander already knew that the message out there to the public—*team*—was the order of the day. He knew that anything that even remotely appeared to be selfish was the furthest thing from any player's best interests, especially his; some had considered Nylander's father to be something less than a team guy, and they would always look for any sign that the same attitude had been passed on as a part of the Nylander DNA.

"We've all taken steps in the right direction," Nylander the younger said. "It was a good year, and we're all looking forward to next year."

It wasn't quite so easy to get off the hook, however. After he talked about how much he had enjoyed playing on a line with Matthews, Nylander was asked if he still considered himself a centre, a short form for centrepiece. He had to suppress a smile and a laugh before he found the right line: in the service of the team. "Wherever the coach wants me to play, I'll play," he said.

Every team has an openly declared code, or bond, and a never-discussed internal web of competing interests. As much as you vow that beating the other guys is your sole motivation, you must first establish your place on the team before going on to fight the good fight. The Maple Leafs were intriguing not just because they were so young and talented this season but because they had three players whose games and skill sets overlapped. For the team to stay together, many players would have to dine on their ego—either Marner or Nylander or both would have to chew and swallow hard the fact that there are only so many slots on the depth chart reserved for centres. Matthews doubtlessly had one, and they would be in competition for another, with no guarantee who would win. Fans could look forward to watching it play out on the ice in coming seasons, but they could only imagine how it would manifest on a psychic level.

The other rookies took their turns in the spotlight. Well, Nikita Zaitsev not so much. He did little more than walk through the room. If he stopped for too long, he would have to face questions that could only hurt him—namely, questions about his contract negotiations. The deal had been in the works for weeks, seemingly agreed to in principle but not finalized. When Zaitsev had taken the heavy hit from Nick Foligno in Game 82, the hit that put him on the sidelines for the first two games of the Washington series, it had to have been a worrisome time.

Kasperi Kapanen and Connor Brown were on either side of the dressing room—exactly how their immediate futures were going to play out would be a compelling subplot. There were some parallels between the two. Both played right wing. Kapanen had scored the goal against the Penguins that had all but kept the Leafs' playoff hopes alive, Brown the goal that clinched a spot in the postseason.

But the parallels extended only so far. Kapanen had been called up from the Marlies late in the season and would be rejoining them for the playoffs, while Brown was done putting in time in the AHL. By now they were in very different places. Though Brown had 20 goals on the season, he had to wonder if there would be a place for him down the line—he was twenty-four, due a new contract, and seemingly fairly close to his ceiling. By contrast, Kapanen was just twenty and, while he had his frustrations with injury, he was buoyed by his showing in his late-season call-up. It was unclear whether there would be room for both of them after next year's camp.

Among the rookies in the room, perhaps Zach Hyman had the best vantage point on the season. Hyman had not been the centre of attention all season, but he had played beside him throughout. Hyman's place with the team wasn't assured like Matthews's, and his prospects in the league were not as bright as Marner's or Nylander's. He was a rookie somehow cast in a journeyman's role, a support player, a grinder—it would be unfair to say that he had hit his ceiling, but if he jumped too high, he'd bump his head. Further, he didn't have a contract, and anything that he might sign with the club would be on terms that would have to accommodate a team that was looking to invest heavily in its other young stars. But despite all that, he was the most visibly excited of the rookies that day.

For Hyman, this wasn't ending. This was just starting over. His contract was going to get done, he said. He gave the impression that he'd pay to play for his home team, or at least rent the ice.

"I'll take a few weeks, visit family I have in California, but then I'll get back to it," he said. "I'll go out to the MasterCard Centre to train with the team's staff and start working towards next year. I'm just excited to have been a part of all this. It was like a dream a lot of the time."

This is what he had signed on for—or at least, when he signed, this was what he had allowed himself to hope for. Any lifelong fan of the team would have to think of it in those terms—allowing yourself to hope.

It's unfair to Hyman to say he led a charmed life with the team as a rookie. It had to be more than a spin of the wheel that landed him on a line with Matthews, had to be more than just being a favourite of the coach to put him on the phenom's wing every game. Maybe it's a little fairer to say that good fortune landed him in the organiza- tion. NHL veterans log hundreds of games to gain access to the free market in their late twenties, but Hyman was there at twenty-two. He had opted for Toronto when it certainly wasn't a widely desired destination for free agents.

It was easy for Hyman, a children's book author, to see a through- line to the season. He didn't have to stretch to reach for it as a personal narrative. "I write stuff that I hope inspires kids," he said. "Maybe the story we wrote here inspires kids who are fans of the team. I know it inspired me."

ACKNOWLEDGMENTS

I couldn't have written the story of the Maple Leafs' season without the help of many people, and hopefully I'll flag most, if not all, in here. If I've missed you, it's an oversight, not a snub, but still, feel free to file your complaints with the customer-service department.

I could not have written this story without the support and, more to the point, the tolerance of the folks at Sportsnet—most notably my bosses Dan Tavares and John Grigg, along with Mike Cormack and Gary Melo. My colleagues in the stable of Sportsnet writers were great sounding boards and contributed in ways that they probably will never fully appreciate, led by Ryan Dixon, Kristina Rutherford, and Dan Robson. Likewise, Evan Rosser and Craig Battle have dry-cleaned and steam-pressed my copy these last six years, and their advice is always therapeutic, as it was here. Chris Johnston, Sportsnet's Leafs beat writer, was generous with his help and great to work beside last season. So, too, was his wingman, Luke Fox.

I am lucky to have friends who've been around the team for many seasons. Dishing out the thanks and props with cause: to Kevin McGran of the *Star*, we'll always have that scenic drive across the Florida swamplands; to Postmedia's Mike Zeisberger, you'll always have the front seat on that scenic drive across the Florida swamplands; to Postmedia's Terry Koshan and the *Hockey News*'s Ken Campbell, you kept me sane and made me laugh too many times to count on those long days at the rink.

ACKNOWLEDGMENTS

Some of my friends from bygone days aren't on the hockey beat anymore, but they always had air for my tires, including Hockey Hall of Famers Frank Orr and Red Fisher and two friends, Jim Kelley and Jim Kernaghan, who didn't quite live to see the day when a Leafs rookie scored four goals in his first NHL game. I think of each of them every day, and they remain big influences on me.

Players, friends, parents, coaches, and agents all more than chipped in over the course of the winter and the spring. If you've reached this point in the book, you'll know just how important all were, because, as a reporter and a writer, I'm on the sidelines. You bring this story alive.

I must thank my editor, Brendan May of Simon & Schuster Canada, who stuck with me and effectively got this book done—some authors will claim to have written books on the fly, day by day, but this one was, in the last strokes, period by period. On the last Saturday night of the regular season, shift by shift in the third period, Brendan saved my bacon. It's really *our* book, even if my name is on the jacket.

My agent, Chris Bucci, called me cold last fall and mentioned that S & S was looking for a book on the Leafs' season. Thank you, Chris, for thinking of me for the project.

And finally, I have to thank my franchise centre, Susan Bourette, and my two favourite wingers, Ellen and Laura. All three of you are two-hundred-foot players, and I'd put the three of you out to take the opening face-off in overtime.